The Greys are the most commonly reported alien species interacting with Earth's inhabitants. *Fifty Shades of Greys* are the true adventures of a four-decade Wright-Patterson Air Force Base scientist searching for evidence of their alien visitation.

Fifty Shades of Greys

*   *   *   *   *   *   *   *   *

Evidence of Extraterrestrial Visitation to Wright-Patterson Air Force Base and Beyond

*   *   *   *   *   *   *   *   *

RAYMOND SZYMANSKI

All photos contained herein are property of the author or were used with the kind permission of their owners as shown below.

Honeycomb Metal: Art Campbell/Chuck Wade
IUFOC Dinner: Jennifer Stein
NatGeo Tree Aerial Photo: Jennifer Stein
Orbs near WPAFB: Jason Hyman
Paul Davids & Al: Paul Davids
Szymanski Children: Stella and Raymond Szymanski Sr.

First Edition. Version 8 April 2016.

This book is dedicated to the Extraterrestrial Phenomena researchers and experiencers whose demonstrated strength inspired me to write this humble contribution to the ever deepening pool of visitation evidence. And to my family and friends whom I saw winking every time I said one of the following: alien, extraterrestrial, abduction, hybrid, and implant, Wright-Patt, ET or UFO – please note, my vision is perfect, it's my hearing that's suspect.

Contents

Foreword

"A journey of a thousand miles must begin with a first step."
Lao-tzu, ancient Chinese philosopher.

      Winter nights in industrial 1960's Detroit were wickedly cold and endlessly dark. The icy winds gave factory workers generous whiffs of acrid assembly plant smoke as they numbly filed in and out of the blue collar corner bars, trying to escape the day's toils. Large Catholic families were comfortably housed nearby in two story wood-framed homes, most with spacious unheated basements. When the factory worker children weren't skating on makeshift backyard ice rinks, they were in their basements playing tennis ball hockey imitating their favorite Detroit Red Wings.

      My brother and I loved tennis ball hockey. My hand speed served me well deflecting his crisp slap shots with my makeshift cardboard blocker. Unfortunately, a missed ball meant that it hit the brick wall behind me with a loud, house-shaking thwack, leaving a bit of tennis ball fuzz behind and annoying parents upstairs. When my dad could no longer concentrate on his beloved *Gunsmoke* television show he would invite us to take a break, "or else!" That's when I would repair to the back porch and stare into the cold night sky from a perch on the handrail, hoping to see something unusual up in space.

      It was the dawn of the '60's and the great space race between the Soviet Union and the United States was at full gallop. By this time both countries had already taken pot shots at the moon using rockets with the Soviets scoring a bull's-eye in September of 1959. Both had also launched unsuspecting pets into space when the Soviets cunningly convinced Laika the dog that the trip she was about to take was not to the vets. Those Rooskies have always been tricksters.

Foreword

Typical Catholic family on back porch in 1960's Detroit. From left to right, Frank, Alan, Ray, Marty. Princess Vicki in front row. My mother insists to this day these were our play clothes. Whatever you say mom, whatever you say. Brother Roy was born too late for this photo.

The US countered with monkeys Able and Baker, who months before had been minding their own business in a quiet corner of a Miami, Florida pet shop. They were launched into the heavens and successfully recovered in 1959. A great moment in US space exploration history, this event was commemorated with the famous saying "Beware of free bananas!"

My extensive experience with the advanced physics of high velocity tennis balls ricocheting around the basement qualified me to naively speculate that some of the rockets we were shooting *up* may come back *down*. Or, we might just be annoying someone up there who had a few spare rockets of their own, and who would be more than happy to repay the favor. Fortunately, all those long nights on the back porch did not produce any returning rockets, friendly or otherwise, only an occasional shooting star or Earth-made orbiting object. My early sky watching days ended abruptly when we mercifully moved out of Detroit in 1968, a year after the 12th Street riots. People in the suburbs kept their porch lights on, obfuscating the night sky but making it easier to spot intruders who wandered north of 8 Mile Road. Though I'd hoped for a close encounter, that event would have to wait, but surprisingly not too much longer. And it was not the type I was looking for.

In January 1973, Dayton, Ohio was experiencing the beginning of what was to be a very mild winter. Detroiters would look upon that weather as Camelot-like where one inch of morning snow would be melted into harmless puddles by 2 pm. It was the beginning of my four decade engineering career at Wright-Patterson Air Force Base and the weather was most appealing for this Michigan refugee. Yes, *that* Wright-Patterson Air Force Base, the reputed hiding place of the 1947 Roswell UFO crash wreckage.

I was assigned to the Avionics Laboratory's Management Operations Office to work with Al, an industrial engineering and MBA graduate who eventually enjoyed a long and very successful civilian career for the US Air Force, at its highest levels. That Al would have such a stellar career was a crazy thought, much like the ones that filled his youthful head as he tooled around in his stress-cracked, Army green Corvette in the early part of the '70s.

During my very first week of work at the legendary Wright-Patterson Air Force Base, Al provided me with some totally unexpected and unsolicited sage advice as we advanced upon the building's "greasy spoon" cafe. With a big brother smile on his face we had the following conversation that is indelibly etched in the recesses of my ever fading memory. I've not been the same since.

Al: "Have you heard about our aliens?"

Ray: "What?!"

Al: "You know, the aliens here on the base."

Ray:" I have absolutely no idea what you are talking about." (This is the first moment I began to suspect that base personnel were drinking on duty time.)

Al: "Yeah, there was a flying saucer crash out West and aliens were recovered and brought here along with their machine."

Ray: "Really?" (There was penultimate sarcasm and disbelief in my voice, like when your buddy told you he once ate poop to impress a girl.)

Al:" Yeah, they keep them in the tunnels."

Ray: "We have tunnels?"

Al: "All over the base."

Ray: "Can we go see these aliens in these tunnels?!"

Al: "Not really. "

Ray: "Why not?"

Al: "Because it's a secret. Only a few people are allowed to see this stuff."

Ray:" If it's a secret, how do you know about this?"

Al: "Everybody who works on base knows."

I was stunned. Me, a young co-op student barely into his first week, was now initiated into a small select group of 10,000 people and given their most incredible secret EVER! We have aliens and their craft in *our* tunnels on *our* base! I love this place!

The excitement was too much for me to handle and I proceeded to make a fatal rookie mistake, I mentioned the "S" word a second time in the same conversation. A bit concerned that 10,000 people might not be able to collectively keep the lid on a "secret" as stunning as the one I now held, I had asked one question too many.

Ray: "In light of what you just told me can you please tell me what your definition of 'secret' is?"

Looking at me like *I* had just eaten poop, he responded. "I think that's enough for now. And I am neither 'confirming' nor 'denying' that we have aliens. So we better get back to work."

Indeed, for the next four decades I had dozens if not hundreds of brief conversations regarding the "secret" I'd been given during my first week on base. Most replies were of the nature of what I was initially told "Oh yeah, we have them. They're in the tunnels."

Apparently it's hard to stop a well-founded legend. Just ask the Brits about King Arthur.

I know. You have to ask, "*Are* there tunnels?" Yes, Wright-Patterson has lots of tunnels. I've been in many of them.

Are there secret vaults where aliens and pieces of their craft could be kept? Yes, there are many secret vaults where aliens and their craft *could* be kept at Wright-Patterson. I've been inside many of these *potential* alien storage locations.

And now the million dollar question:" Does Wright-Patterson actually house aliens and their artifacts?"

At this point of writing this book I'm not sure.

According to dozens of current and former base employees I've talked to, military and civilian, General Officer level down to GS-5s, they unanimously agree that Wright-Patterson is the logical location for such items to be evaluated. However, they also agree that if these materials were ever housed at the base it is also logical to think that they have since been moved to other locations for advanced exploitation. I tend to somewhat agree with the consensus, but not entirely.

These opinions notwithstanding, I have not been discouraged from looking at Wright-Patterson and elsewhere for evidence of extraterrestrial life. After all, I encountered lots of intelligent life at the base despite all the negative comments in the media about government employee incompetence. If the media can be so wrong about intelligence in government circles I can't imagine they would miss an opportunity to be dead wrong about the existence of extraterrestrial intelligence.

Let the Quest begin!

Wright-Patt has many buildings that could swallow UFOs up to 150-feet in diameter. Most reported UFOs are less than 100 feet.

Introduction

There are many magnificent places on this planet that attract scads of khaki-clad tourists for obvious reasons. The Grand Canyon, Yellowstone Park, and the Taj Mahal immediately come to mind. Then again there are other super popular sites whose attraction is entirely lost on me.

Underwater caves, the Amazon, and anywhere in India are the most puzzling of all destinations. The point is every destination has some attraction which induces the visitor to abandon the comfort of their sofa and satellite TV and travel halfway across the planet to stare at 15-foot-tall stone columns standing silently in an open field. In Britain of all places! So it is with me and famous Unidentified Flying Object (UFO) incidents.

I'm fascinated by sites associated with UFOs and the extraterrestrial hypotheses because I believe it is one of the most important stories for our planet, ever! Before I take a visit to a site I thoroughly research it until I can close my eyes and see the event happening in real time. Although it is unlikely I will find any remaining physical evidence to make world governments understandably nervous, there is always the possibility I will uncover additional information for future generations to exploit.

With that goal in mind I present photos and essays on many of the most interesting adventures I've enjoyed while searching for that one bit of information that could unlock the UFO mystery. You are invited, no urged, to follow my footsteps, have a look around for yourself and see if you might be the person who finds the golden key. I promise to leave a few tantalizing evidential breadcrumbs along the mysterious UFO trail for you to follow as you begin your own personal journey of discovery.

Adventure 1
Exeter UFO Revisited

Norman Muscarello

Near 2 am on September 3, 1965, eighteen-year-old Norman Muscarello walked down a New Hampshire country road and straight into weird history. He was in rural Kensington hitchhiking on Amesbury Road, aka Route 150, just outside of Exeter. There he encountered a 90-foot, red glowing, blinking UFO hovering over the farm house of Clyde Russell. This was the beginning of one of the best researched and documented UFO encounters in history, involving dozens of witnesses including police officers who saw the craft with Norman.

On October 20, 1965, author John G. Fuller set up his headquarters at The Exeter Inn to begin research for his famous book *Incident at Exeter*. His book meticulously documents Muscarello's historic close encounters with that 90-foot UFO and numerous other contemporary encounters by local area residents over a one year period. Simultaneous eyewitness accounts from multiple police officers, who were with Muscarello during his second close encounter at 3 am on September 3rd, make this site as historically significant to Ufologists as Stonehenge is to modern day Druids. And so it is most worthy as the first step on the thousand mile journey, to a place where the spirit of Norman Muscarello and his encounters are still alive in Exeter, New Hampshire after half a century. I would begin my journey there.

In 2008 I was visiting the Boston area for several days. Since Exeter was only about a one hour drive from where I was staying, it would be extremely convenient for visiting the famous sites of Norman Muscarello's close encounters. Especially intriguing was the seasonal timing of the trip which would be in September, the same month as Norman's experience. In preparation for the trip, Google Earth and Fuller's *Incident at Exeter* became my best lunchtime friends, helping to locate Norman's sighting location somewhere on Route

150 in Kensington, New Hampshire, very near the town of Exeter. I printed a screenshot of the estimated location, placed an "X" in the middle of the field between the Clyde Russell and Carl Dining farms and tucked it safely in my travel folder.

Boston's Logan airport welcomed me on a clear sunny afternoon in September 2008. I was quite familiar with the Boston area since one of my former Air Force projects was contracted to a technology company in Reading, Massachusetts. I had made dozens of trips to the area for regularly scheduled progress reviews and, while waiting for plane departures, visited interesting sites like Fenway Park, Durgin Park (a restaurant with intentionally rude waitresses), the Boston Garden, Cheers, and a list of other historical sites. Despite this over-familiarity with the Boston area, I was genuinely excited about going to Exeter to retrace the footsteps of Fuller, Muscarello and other key characters I'd come to know in *Incident*.

By the time I arrived in Boston I had read John Fuller's book twice and consulted its pages many times in an attempt to identify and select sites important to the Exeter story. At the top of the list were The Exeter Inn where Fuller often resided while researching the story, the Russell and Dining farm location where Muscarello and others had close encounters, and Pease Air Force Base whose personnel provided some unexpected comic relief for these very strange UFO events. I was also curious to see the town of Exeter itself and the police station that recorded hundreds of UFO reports from concerned citizens in the months surrounding the famous sighting. Devoid of any firsthand knowledge of Exeter and its surrounding locales, images of Gomer Pyle running through Mayberry while yelling "citizen's arrest" ran sporadically through my head.

First Visit to The Exeter Inn and Muscarello UFO Site

It was late afternoon when I checked into my hotel. Since I did not have firm plans until the following morning, I grabbed my GPS unit and my camera and headed out for Exeter post haste, feeling like one does on Christmas morning. The evening's plan was to visit The Exeter Inn, have some food and talk to the older locals about their famous UFO history. Then I'd do some quick reconnaissance at the Russell and Dining sites when the sky would be dark and moonless, trying to closely simulate the exact conditions of September 3, 1965, when according to celestial records and contemporary accounts, the moon set three hours prior to Muscarello's first encounter.

My trusty Garmin GPS easily led me to The Exeter Inn at 90 Front Street. I was anxious to step back in time and see what type of environment John Fuller operated in while interviewing witnesses and transcribing hours of testimony in 1965. Perhaps there would be a lingering "period ambience" that could help me better visualize Fuller and his witnesses sitting in the lobby trying to wring every last fact out of their otherworldly experiences. But suddenly, bam! Reality check!

When I entered the *Inn* I couldn't help but notice that there was a widespread renovation in progress with small corners of real estate closed off with tarps and such. Then it hit me. "Houston, we have a problem." This would regrettably not be The Exeter Inn of author John G. Fuller.

After a resigned inquiry I was informed by hotel staff that the exterior Georgian style of the Inn was almost exactly the way it was in 1965. However, the hotel was in the midst of "meticulous renovations and enhancements" authorized by new owners who purchased the Inn in 2007. They were meticulously renovating the entrances, the lobby, the meeting rooms, bedrooms and everything else under the roof. According to the hotel staff, the interior of The Exeter Inn in 2008 was no longer trapped in 1965 when John Fuller interviewed witnesses with his trusty tape recorder. The entire décor was in the process of being changed, albeit "meticulously", a word the new owners had apparently hypnotized the entire staff to use repeatedly.

3

The Exeter Inn exterior looks pretty much as it did in 1965 when it served as the initial headquarters for *Incident at Exeter*'s John G. Fuller.

The now absent 1965 interior ambience would have to be partially resurrected by the memories of locals, including an elderly gentleman I befriended at the bar the following evening. Not only did he have a great recollection of The Exeter Inn, whose bar he visited nightly, but he was old enough to recall the *Incident* and was willing to talk about it. I took a short stroll around the hotel and planned to return the following evening for a closer look at the renovations and more detailed discussions with the meticulously prepared staff.

It was just before 11 pm when I left The Exeter Inn and headed to the Russell and Dining farms which were less than two miles away. There was no other traffic as I pointed my car to southbound Court Street which would take me to the Route 150 cutoff. As I neared what would be the last streetlamp in Exeter, a London fog enveloped the road and my car shown starkly under that last streetlight before being plunged into total darkness. I had to wonder if this was normal weather for September or was some higher force giving me an ominous welcome to a place familiar with cosmic strangeness.

By the time I reached the Route 150 cut off, the town of Exeter had disappeared in my rear view mirror along with anything outside the reach of my headlamps. I slowed the car to a crawl while my GPS dutifully kept me posted on my position. I was amazed at how pitch black it was outside the windows and hoped that the GPS batteries were fully charged. There was no other vehicular traffic anywhere to be seen.

Only Hollywood could have written this script. A spooky, moonless night on a dark country road cloaked in a dense, low-lying, and headlight-choking fog awaited the author. What could possibly go wrong?

As the car approached the intersection of Brewer Road and Route 150, the GPS let me know that I had successfully arrived at my long awaited crossroads. Using a move guaranteed to impress any native Bostonian driver; I turned onto Brewer and made an immediate no-signal U-turn so that I would be facing Route 150 as it ran south to north in the direction of Exeter.

There was plenty of roadside parking there, enough for more than one car. And by the looks of the adjacent worn patches of grass in my headlights, I wasn't the first person to launch a midnight investigation from that exact location.

I carefully eased the car off the asphalt onto the grassy area to minimize the sound of tires crunching the off-road gravel. No need to bring attention to myself at this hour of the night I thought. When the car stopped, the eerie quiet and extreme dark made me more than just a little bit nervous. Not a "good nervous" like asking someone on a date mind you. More like a "bad nervous" when you think they'll reject your offer and send you home in crushing defeat. Not that I've ever felt that before.

Taking a long deep breath I abandoned the safety of the car and began carefully walking along Route 150 toward the Dining and Russell properties now hidden in the night. I unconsciously slipped into Muscarello mode as I made my way past what I believed to be the Dining farmhouse and paused at the open field where Norman first spotted his UFO far in the distance. At that moment, as it was decades earlier, there were no streetlights, no moonlight and no vehicular traffic. This scenario provides three good reasons for being concerned for one's solitary welfare on a lonely road, the absence of a 90-foot hovering UFO notwithstanding.

As I approached what I believed to be the Russell home I imagined a 90-foot, red pulsating orb hovering a few dozen feet overhead. I had to wonder if Muscarello might have reacted stronger than his reported dive into a nearby ditch and his subsequent pounding on the Russell front door for help.

Every possible scenario that I imagined while standing in front of that field next to the Russell home had me sprinting down the road at top speed screaming like a little girl in untied Nikes. Or worse yet, I imagined standing in-place, paralyzed by fear, but still screaming like a little girl. In retrospect that might have been a more effective involuntary strategy than Norman's farmhouse door pounding, which history reveals did not yield a helpful response from the hesitant, sleeping Russell household.

Unable to awaken the Russells at 2am, who thought they had a rowdy drunk on their front porch, Norman was eventually able to flag down a car to take him straight to the Exeter police station. Exactly how he was able to get it together long enough to flag down a car under those circumstances is as big of a mystery to me as the craft he spotted, not once, *but twice* on that fateful night.

Fortunately, I was going to have a lot of time to think about that puzzle while driving back to the hotel and all through the next day's activities. It was getting late and I wanted to be up early in the morning. I fell asleep that night counting UFOs popping up over the Russell house as I reacted like a cleanly struck whack-a-mole target. Could it have been something I ate?

The Exeter Inn welcomed the author in 2008.

Arthur Russell: Son of Clyde Russell, Exeter Witness

Late the next day I found myself heading back to the Exeter area and parking again at the intersection of Route 150 and Brewer Road to continue my investigation in the shadow of the Russell and Dining farms, home to the Muscarello UFO sightings. My mind was still processing the prior day's viewing of the UFO encounter site, a location I had thought about visiting for years.

With more time now available, my new plan was to visit the Muscarello site in the daylight to establish that I had indeed found the real site in preparation for a return later that evening. I had long imagined walking down Route 150 on a moonless night to see how dark it actually was in that location in 1965, imagining the appearance of a 90-foot, glowing red, hovering object. I also wanted to knock on the Russell's front door; much like Muscarello did 43 years prior, minus the soiled pants and uncontrolled panic of course.

Brewer Road and Route 150. Nearby Muscarello encountered a UFO in 1965. The author had a strange nighttime encounter here in 2008.

After parking the car at Brewer Road and Route 150, I took several photos of the general area including the field where the sightings took place near the Dining and Russell homes. I returned to

8

my car and decided to visit the home that, to the best of my knowledge, belonged to the Russells in 1965. I didn't come all this way just to lay up as they say in championship golf.

Was this the former home of Clyde Russell of *Incident at Exeter* fame?

The thing is, I wasn't 100 percent sure if the driveway I was about to enter was *the* Clyde Russell driveway or not. Granted, I had spent many hours of research piecing together clues that led me to choosing what I thought was the actual locations of the sighting and the Dining and Russell farm locations. I had a map with an "X" on it, but I'd put it there. And I was mindful of Indiana Jones' warning that "X never marks the spot", unless of course you're beating a hole in a library floor located somewhere in Venice.

As I cautiously entered the driveway, neatly framed by the house and the detached garage, I was excited to see a large "R" on the aluminum screen front door. Could this actually be the former home of Clyde Russell who was made famous in John Fuller's book just because a large unidentified flying object illuminated his property all those decades ago?!

Due to my pre-visit research I knew that Clyde Russell who owned the home during the *Incident* passed away in 1969 at the age of 70. So climbing up the porch stairs I had to wonder if the home was still owned by a Russell relative or did the current owner conveniently have a last name that began with the letter, "R"? I gave the aluminum door three quick knocks and waited for an answer to that mission-critical question.

While pacing nervously for a response on that beautiful mid-September afternoon, I began to hear a whirring, muffled mechanical sound slowly approaching my position. Oh, oh! Am I about to be "experienced" in the shadow of Exeter? Are they back? As I thought about the problem of leaving this planet at a most inconvenient time, the sound soon grew loud enough for me to realize that the abduction vehicle would have been a tractor.

Almost immediately an elderly man came into view driving a small front loader which was full of late-summer garden vegetation. He was not wearing the tight-fitting silvery outfits ascribed to alien visitors but rather the quintessential fashion combo of a well-dressed gentlemen farmer: light-blue long-sleeved denim shirt, dark blue Dickies pants with suspenders, and aviator sunglasses, all regally topped off with a Home Depot ball cap. If that front loader had wings he would have been flying it in style.

I slowly came down the steps and walked across the grass, making sure to hold my large camera high enough for my new found friend to easily see it. I wanted to put him at ease as an unannounced stranger approached his vehicle. Experience has taught me that most folks recognize a professional camera as the tool of an educated, sophisticated gentleman. OK, maybe a little over the top, but seeing my camera assured the driver that I wasn't there for any nefarious purpose. The farmer climbed out of his vehicle and immediately gave me a bone crunching New England farmer handshake. Welcome to Exeter, greenhorn!

Arthur Russell met the author in true New England gentleman farmer fashion, with the business end of a front loader tractor. With a history of UFOs hovering over his home I suspect this would be his weapon of choice for the next encounter.

With a wry smile, eighty-year-old Arthur Russell listened patiently as I told him about the *Incident at Exeter* and how this journey was more of a religious pilgrimage for me than a social visit. For the next ten minutes I excitedly regaled him with my intimate knowledge of Muscarello minutia, rattling off a detailed timeline of events and in-depth character descriptions known only to the ufologically disturbed.

When I finally surfaced to take a gulp of air, Arthur used that microsecond of silence to casually point to the area directly over the house and said "That's where they saw it." Suddenly, my unassailable knowledge of Norman Muscarello and his UFO seemed about as useful as a screen door on a submarine.

Stunned into silence, I learned that in 1965, Arthur and his family lived on the property next to his father, *the* Clyde Russell, about 100 yards up the road on Route 150. Arthur gave me his recollection of the story, including the fact that his father did not answer the door because he feared the man on the porch was "just a drunk", and hoped that drunk would just wander off into the night. So much for farmer's intuition!

According to Arthur Russell and other event reports, this photo reflects where Norman Muscarello was standing when he encountered a UFO hovering above the Clyde Russell home at 2 am on September 3, 1965.

Arthur said that Norman encountered the unidentified craft just as the Russell home and garage came into his view. According to Arthur's sources at the time, Norman briefly dropped down next to the nearby stone wall before making a dash to the other side of the street because Norman thought he was about to be landed upon. In his haste in the black of night Norman tripped and fell into the shallow ditch on the other side of the road where he stayed until the object retreated. Shortly thereafter Norman began his fruitless pounding on the Russell front door that went unanswered, thus depriving the Russells of a chance for an up close and personal encounter of their own.

Arthur then offered to show me around the scene-of-the-crime and I was only too happy to oblige. This was *so* much better than the trespassing episode I was planning if my knocks on the front door went unanswered, like those of Norman Muscarello decades before.

Although he was eighty-years-young on the day I spent with Arthur Russell he was as sharp as a tack and as strong as a bull. Here he was describing the entire first encounter of Norman Muscarello in detail, including Norman's short lived hiding behind the stone "wall", his dive across the street and his knocking on the Russell door.

The Russell property runs southwest to northeast from the front to the back. Arthur showed me the open area adjoining his property where he believed the craft camped out in between its terrorizing flights around the neighborhood. Although Arthur claimed that he was not interested in UFO's beyond the one that hovered over his childhood home, he did point out the large electric transmission lines that divided his land from the open field beyond. He'd heard that the craft chose to rest there because it provided a concealed, refueling energy source. Arthur also pointed out water retention areas that he mused could be used to top off the alien craft's radiator. We stood there for a moment in complete agreement, staring up at the large electrical supply cables and contemplating those most logical possibilities.

This is the northern tip of the Russell property. 200 feet away, on the other side of large trees, are set of high voltage power lines and a huge meadow which would serve as an ideal hiding spot for the large craft seen by Muscarello and two police officers in the immediate area.

Our next stop was the stone wall Norman hid near during his first sighting. Maybe it was my imagination, but I had envisioned a wall tall enough for Muscarello to actually *gain refuge* from the glowing, 90-foot orb. The stone "wall" Arthur showed me was only three feet tall at its highest point, hardly a wall worthy of a Mel Gibson-inspired, Braveheart-like siege.

The large, angular, lichen covered rocks in the wall would most certainly halt a speeding Volkswagen dead in its tracks. But it's doubtful that they would provide a safe haven from intergalactic marauders cruising around in a giant spacecraft. When I pointed out this problem to Arthur he took pause and then sagely replied "Maybe it was taller back then."

According to Arthur Russell and other published sources, Muscarello originally sought shelter behind these large boulders until he realized he was still being illuminated by the craft. He then bolted across the street, tripping in the process, and found himself face down in a shallow ditch next to the road.

Arthur was most generous with his time and knowledge but he kept mentioning that he was going to a local bingo. Taking this as a cue to wrap-it-up I took a few photos by the stone wall with Arthur on the exact spot where Norman hid on his first encounter. Basking in the warm sunshine in broad daylight and discussing events that happened decades ago, the Muscarello's stone wall refuge did not seem like such a scary place after all.

From my car I retrieved a copy of *Incident at Exeter* which Arthur happily autographed and dated. I thanked Arthur for his time and wished him good luck at bingo, fully intending on heading directly into Exeter and doing some more research before having dinner at The Exeter Inn. As I turned to the car I was stopped in my tracks. "Would you like to meet someone who owned the Carl Dining farm next door shortly after Muscarello's sighting?" Arthur said, matter-of-factly.

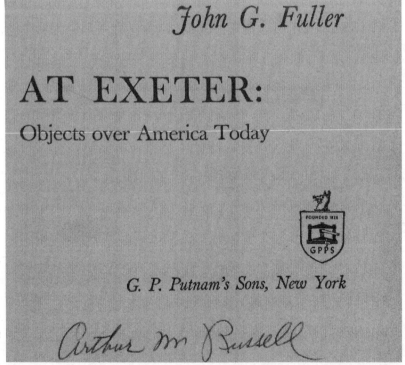

Arthur Russell autographed one of the author's copies of *Incident at Exeter*. The author donated a pristine first edition of the book to the local library in the author's town to ensure future generations' access.

High Hopes for Arthur Russell's Friends

Arthur hopped into my car and within a minute we were turning off Route 150 onto Moulton Ridge Road, heading down a heavily tree-lined road to a gravel driveway which led to a classic New England style wood clad, two-story home. Total commute time was about three minutes. A tail wagging people-friendly dog met us as the car pulled to a stop and Arthur proceeded to the back door to alert the owners of our presence. I kept a wary eye on the dog in the unlikely event he bore the name of CUJO and hadn't been fed in a while.

Shortly thereafter I found myself introduced to Arthur's friends: Stephen and Ann, a married couple I surmised were in their late sixties. They led us to seats next to their garden and we were soon in a conversation about small acreage farming, bee keeping and yes, bingo. Arthur told his friends that I was visiting the area to learn more about the "1965 UFO sighting" and that he brought me to their home in hopes that they would share their experiences with me while they owned the Dining Farm..

I started the UFO conversation with Stephen and Ann by describing Muscarello's first encounter at the Clyde Russell home and his second encounter an hour later, in a field next to the Russell property which was owned by Carl Dining. Surprisingly, Stephen and Ann both denied having anything but an elementary knowledge of the *Incident*, despite the fact that they had owned and lived in the former Carl Dining home from 1970 until 1978.

Stephen explained that in 1965, the year of the Muscarello sighting, he was living and teaching at Philips Exeter Academy in Exeter. He was married with two children and a wife. And despite the fact that Norman Muscarello's encounter, and the encounters of many other locals, were being detailed in the local newspaper, Stephen was totally unaware of those events at that time. It wasn't until he read John Fuller's *Incident at Exeter*, years later, that he became aware of the events heralded therein.

After reading Fuller's book, Stephen said that he and Ann became "very vigilant" about all things in the skies. Despite those many decades of vigilance in the very neighborhood of Muscarello's sighting, Stephen claims that neither he nor his wife can recall seeing anything in the skies they could not easily explain.

While living in the former Carl Dining home for several years, Stephen was aware of the many post-Incident visitations to his field by UFO researchers and other interested parties. He recalled that the human visitations to the "Muscarello site" reached their peak long before he bought the property in 1970, though they were recorded in the local newspapers.

The field located between the Clyde Russell and Carl Dining properties where Norman Muscarello and two Exeter Police Officers, Eugene Bertrand and David Hunt, encountered a 90-foot, red glowing object hovering as close as 100 feet overhead on 3 September 1965.

To the best of his recollection, he had but a single encounter with an individual awaiting a return of the space brothers to the Dining Farm. It was on an anniversary of the original encounter in the early Seventies. The one-person intergalactic welcoming committee was hanging out at the #668 utility pole near the sighting field made famous in the Fuller book. The nighttime visitor told Stephen that he was "waiting for the ship to return".

Not sensing any imminent personal threat from this peaceful group-of-one, when it was time for bed Stephen closed the house lights and hit the sack. The visitor was gone by daybreak. Whether they departed on foot, in a car, or by the anticipated spaceship is unknown at this time. Stephen was also unsure of where this fellow hailed from or what his name was, having not obtained that information when they briefly met.

One fact Stephen *was* sure of was the extraordinary damage that Carl Dining's horses did to their stable on the night of the Muscarello encounter. According to multiple witnesses who viewed the damage, it was well beyond the normal wear and tear expected within the confines of a horse stable. The damage was so extensive and unusual that one well-informed neighbor, Clark Jacobs, took to telling all his friends about it. As one can imagine, in a small community like post-Incident Kensington, this story found its way back to the owner of the Dining Farm, Stephen Smith!

Sensing that Stephen and Ann had more to add to their story than barn damage, I pressed them again about personal sightings. As a result, Stephen unexpectedly and coarsely said "Arthur, you know I don't like talking about this!" He then excused himself with an apology of "having to attend to some things". After shooting Arthur what appeared to be a "you really inconvenienced me with your visitor" look, he went to his car and departed for parts unknown. Apparently my aggressive questioning was the New England equivalent of dropping a Baby Ruth in the proverbial punch bowl.

On the way home, Arthur again apologized for his friends less-than-helpful behavior. He was certain, he said, that Stephen and Ann had more to add to the story and was as confused as I was to experience this rather unfriendly reaction. What we thought was going to be a great first-person revelation turned out to be an unexpected early dismissal.

I thanked Arthur once again for an enlightening afternoon, we said our good-byes, and I pointed the car north on Route 150. I was going to search for the old Exeter Police Station at its 1965 location and have a leisurely walk around the town. I wanted to get a sense of what is was like all those years ago when Norman Muscarello burst into the station with an unbelievable story which fortunately for posterity was actually believed by the desk officer, Reginald "Scratch" Toland.

In 1965 this was the entrance to the Exeter Police Station. This is where Officer Toland would have heard Norman Muscarello's first report of his close encounter with a 90-foot UFO.

Norman Muscarello and the Town of Exeter

My first stop was the original Exeter police station where Norman Muscarello burst in and blurted out his incredible story to Officer "Scratch" Toland. He told Toland he was hitchhiking home on Route 150 when he had a terrifying close encounter with an extremely bright, large glowing object. When the object retreated to the rear property of the nearby farmhouse Norman told Scratch that he unsuccessfully tried to awaken the family who owned the home by pounding repeatedly on their front door. He then jumped in front of the first car he saw heading into Exeter, one that kindly took him directly to the station.

The police station in 1965 was ensconced in the lower level of the Exeter Town Hall at 9 Front Street, exactly where one would expect to house a police department in a small New Hampshire town. It was nestled amongst the storefronts, close to its citizens and its heartbeat. Downtown Exeter in 2008 looks like it did in 1965, giving you a good sense of what Exeter was like when UFOs were buzzing its citizens in the town's dark outskirts.

2008 downtown Exeter, viewed from the 1965 Police Station location.

21

As Officer Toland was debriefing Norman around 2:30 am, another officer, Eugene Bertrand, reported that a woman he spoke to claimed to have been harassed in her car by a low-flying, brilliantly-glowing red object that followed her. With this supporting information, Officer Toland thought it prudent to send Officer Bertrand and Norman back to Norman's sighting location in the hopes of disproving Norman's claim and giving him a chance to calm down. If disproving Norman's story and calming him down was *"the plan"* then it couldn't have gone more wrong for the Exeter police.

The Exeter Town Hall housed the small Police Department in cramped quarters in 1965. After Muscarello's story became widespread the office was besieged for months with UFO reports by locals who were no longer afraid of potential ridicule.

By 3 am, Officer Bertrand and Muscarello were roaming around the field that separated the Dining and Russell farms. Bertrand parked the car next to pole #668, now replaced and renumbered as VZ 34S. They walked down to a corral 75-100 yards from the road. Horses at the farm began to kick and vocalize while nearby dogs began barking. As the object rose slowly from behind the tree line Muscarello screamed, "I see it! I see it!"

Bertrand turned to see it too and he immediately dragged Muscarello back to the patrol car "afraid of infrared rays or radiation." He radioed Toland back at the station announcing "I see it myself!" The object hovered for several minutes before moving away toward Hampton, just long enough for late arriving Patrolman Dave Hunt to share the sighting with Bertrand and Muscarello. When it arrived in Hampton a minute later, a man located there called the Exeter operator to report a low flying UFO that matched the descriptions of the other witnesses. Bingo!

By 1979 the Exeter Police Department had grown proportionately to the town and they relocated to new quarters at 20 Court Street where they remain to this day. More significantly, it was only a half mile from there to The Exeter Inn for my return visit, dinner and a few surprises.

The desk sergeant I talked to in September 2008 had absolutely no recollection of the Exeter UFO. When I asked, they offered that police records from that time period would have been destroyed long ago.

Chasing History at The Exeter Inn

When I arrived at The Exeter Inn for dinner it was early evening and most of the newly remodeled restaurant's tables were already filled with couples or groups. I settled in at the bar, asked for a menu and ordered a classic Southern Comfort Manhattan on the rocks. It seemed appropriate at the time to revisit the *Inn's* golden era with a vintage cocktail.

Sitting at the new bar one can see the entire meticulously refurbished restaurant. The image of the alien-looking GEICO Gecko attacking the bartender is purely coincidental.

The bar started to fill up quickly as I nursed my drink and opened my camera to review the day's accomplishments. At about that point a very well dressed octogenarian sat next to me and asked what I was doing with such an expensive camera. His name was Russell Fieldsend and I was to learn he was well qualified to identify expensive cameras since he had spent many years as a model in New York after World War II.

By 1965 Mr. Fieldsend had returned to Exeter to help his parents with their thriving dry cleaning business, eventually opening his own store a few short years later. He was also an accomplished pianist playing in local restaurants, bars and clubs, evenings and on weekends. Both his day job and nighttime hobby gave him regular interaction with the public in and around Exeter, often a public eager to discuss the rash of UFO sightings from years ago. It was inevitable that Mr. Fieldsend would be subjected to a flow of UFO stories from his dry cleaning customers and the piano enthusiasts who attended his performances.

Appearing as though he is attracting new age "energy orbs" 80-years-young piano impresario Russell Fieldsend shared his recollections of the Exeter UFO incident and his career while sipping martinis at The Exeter Inn. Russell revealed that the secret to his longevity was, of course, the nightly Martinis.

Arthur related to me that the whole Exeter UFO incident was "quite the thing" and certainly the topic of the day for several weeks. Although he claims he did not have a personal encounter with the UFO, he did meet several people who did and who shared their stories with him. Unfortunately, at eighty-years-young he apologized for not being able to recall specific names and more details of what he heard, but he was well aware of the lingering community-wide impact of the sightings and Fuller's *Incident*.

Dinner arrived and Russell kept me company for the duration, slowly draining his martini and entertaining me with his exploits from another era. When I was finally able to derail his history train he was keen to describe the former glory of The Exeter Inn, including the restaurant area which was in full view. Based on his extensive descriptions, and his positive opinion of the renovations, I didn't miss much "ambience" as the time-worn hotel was long overdue for the current remodeling.

After bidding Russell a fond adieu and thanking him for his recollections I decided to snoop about the hotel and talk to more staff before heading out for a night visit to the Muscarello site. The friendly front desk receptionist wanted nothing to do with UFO talk and pointed me in the direction of the hotel management office, temporarily located in the conference center. Although I was totally unannounced, three young management types were more than happy to entertain a discussion of my visit and provided me surprising recollections related to the incident.

The first revelation they shared was printed on a sign attached to the wall directly behind me. There one could find the names of the Inn's four meeting rooms: Squamscott, Gilman, Pennacook, and Fuller. One young manager verified that the Fuller room was indeed named after John Fuller, the author of *Incident at Exeter*, but deferred to her colleagues in identifying the other namesakes. As I later discovered, along with their exceptional scholarship, all were spared the harshness of a public school education.

According to my three youthful scholars, the Squamscott and Pennacook rooms were named after two local area Native American tribes who were strongly related to each other. They were two of the first tribes to encounter European colonists and thus were two of the first tribes to be decimated by introduced diseases. This historical moment spawned the famous phrase "Beware of free blankets" which would have been great advice for the natives to heed before taking said blankets.

As for the name Gilman, they have been one of the most prominent families in the entire history of Exeter, taking political leadership positions there for centuries. Yes, centuries. There is even a popular home-turned-museum in Exeter named after Colonel Nicholas Gilman who served as the treasurer for New Hampshire from 1775 until his death in 1783. His accomplished children, one who became Governor, were raised in that home and it stayed in the family for decades. With this knowledge my faith in America's often beleaguered education system had been fully restored and I was ready to enter the night.

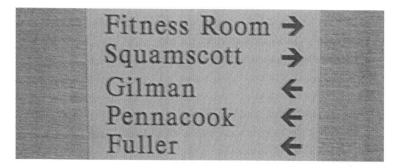

Despite not being decimated like the local Native American Squamscott and Pennacook tribes, nor serving as a New Hampshire Governor like John Gilman, author John Fuller still managed to get a meeting room named in his honor at The Exeter Inn.

I headed to my car and flipped on the GPS. I was taking a slightly modified route which would have me driving past an area known as Shaw's Hill which figures prominently as another frequent UFO sighting location in Fuller's book. I didn't expect to see anything at Shaw's Hill in the dark of night - but then again - the darker it is the easier to see large glowing airborne objects.

Unforgettably Surreal Nighttime Encounter

Heading southbound on Route 150, about one quarter mile short of the Muscarello encounter site, I took the Shaw Hill Road cutoff on my right and followed that for about a quarter mile, then turned left onto Brewer Road heading to Route 150 about a quarter mile in the distance. I was expecting to park in the same off-road location on Brewer as I had done peacefully twice before, but apparently the local residents or government agents had other ideas.

As the car crept toward the intersection of Brewer and Route 150, easing the car off the road, my car's headlamps suddenly illuminated a gigantic, ten-foot tall, yellow hulking monster. I hit the brakes. My tires tried to take hold but were no match for the crunching sliding gravel underneath. As I rapidly approached the monster I could only think of how I would explain the damage to the rental car agency. The car stopped. My heart raced. I faced the monster.

The windows in the car were rolled down and not one sound could be heard. I waited a minute or so before leaving the car to enter the pitch dark night to confront the huge beast that had nearly sent me into a panic. When I got close enough to identify it I could not come up with an explanation as to who, why or how it had come to rest in my planned parking spot.

Imagine my surprise when I found a Komatsu WA250 Wheel Loader occupying the precise location I had used the previous evening to visit the Russell and Dining farm locations. This bright yellow beast is ten and a half feet tall, twenty three feet long and eight feet wide with reflective stickers sprinkled liberally over its surface. This was the last thing I expected to encounter on this night in this location and I began to speculate conspiratorially.

Had one of the local farmers moved this giant machine here to thwart my convenient visits to the 1965 encounter site? Was this connected in any way to Steven's unexpected outburst and sudden fleeing of my questions just the afternoon prior? Whoever did this for whatever reason, I soon discovered clear evidence they had some government help in doing so.

Firmly affixed to the WA250 was a very large "New Hampshire DOT" reflective sign, blue letters on white background, conspicuously located on the driver's cab. As I circled the area with my camera the government conspiracy explanation started to pick up traction. I noticed that the WA250 was bracketed, front and back, with separate, large DOT auxiliary equipment. These were a road widener blade and a street sweeper attachment each occupying several additional feet of space.

WTF! Maybe it was the fact that I had told the locals I worked for the US Air Force that caused them to show me absolutely no respect by dumping tons of immoveable objects into what was clearly the roadside parking place from which I was conducting my investigation.

Supporting my rapidly developing conspiracy theory is the fact that these additional pieces of road equipment guaranteed that the level parking places next to the road were nearly 100% occupied by the machinery. As a result, visitors now had to park amongst the weeds and trees and prepare themselves to explain the vehicular scratches to the rental car company. While contemplating just such an encounter for the next morning I pulled my camera from my backpack and departed the car to take a few photos, including one of the beast as evidence.

I returned to the car to gather my thoughts and sort through the real meaning of this unexpected surprise. Although it was earlier in the evening than the previous night's visit, it was just as dark, if not darker. I was just about to remove the key from the car's ignition and go for a site visit when I received one final Exeter surprise. This one would surpass by far anything I had already experienced in the land of Muscarello, my very own close encounter.

Leaning slightly forward and looking out the windshield, I noticed a light moving slowly from the upper right corner of the glass to the center of the windshield. As the light disappeared behind the front loader parked forward of my car, I waited for the light to reappear in the left side of the windshield, fully expecting that it was a car heading north on Route 150. That light never reappeared.

About the time the "car" should have passed Brewer Road where I was parked I began to hear it slowly approaching my position – with its headlights obviously off! It was so dark I could not see it approaching but I could clearly hear it. My fight or flight reflex was now in high gear because I was stuck behind the monstrous loader without a fast escape route. What did I get myself into I wondered? My heart continued to pick up speed until I heard *the* voice. Then I nearly freaked.

The approaching car stopped so the driver's window was opposite mine – I think. I still could not see the other vehicle but made this positional assumption when its driver started to talk – directly to me! The voice was within several feet, maybe closer, and seemed to come directly across from me. In the middle of the absolute pitch dark night this is the conversation I had with a disembodied voice only yards from Muscarello's 1965 sighting.

The woman's voice was confident and very professional, sounding like that of a television prosecuting attorney. I would guesstimate she was approximately 40 to 50 years of age.

Woman: "Hi there." (Spoken like you would expect a lunch date to sound.)

Me: "Hi." (Spoken like someone who just soiled his pants.)

Woman: "What are you doing here?"

Recall, it is so dark I can neither see the person nor their car, if it even was a car! And this "woman" is interrogating me in the middle of the night on a lonely country road! If I can't see her, I'm pretty sure she cannot see me - and I'd been sitting there a while so my eyes were as adjusted to the dark as they could be.

Me: "Well, I'm visiting the area for a few days investigating the famous UFO sightings that took place here in 1965. I'm visiting the sights mentioned in the Fuller book and taking some pictures."

Woman: "You know they're not coming back." (Totally ignoring *everything* that I had just said to her.)

Me: "Yeah, I know that but I'm just trying to get a feeling of what it was like as Muscarello walked down this lonely country road in total darkness."

Woman: "You're wasting your time. There's nothing here to see. They're not coming back."

At this point it was clear that I was not welcome in the local area by the mystery voice, nor the New Hampshire Department of Transportation, and who knew *how many* others. I was relieved that I was still alive and began to think about how to segue out of the conversation and my captive parking spot. Then again, I had come too far to leave with unanswered questions so I decided to roll the dice.

Me: "What makes you think they're not coming back?

Woman: "They're not coming back."

Me: "Are you sure?"

Woman: "I'm sure."

I couldn't argue with her conviction, but her proof left something to desire.

Sometimes you roll the dice and come up snake eyes. This was the case here. But I was still breathing.

Now I had even more questions - like "who the hell are you?" and "what the hell are you doing out here questioning strangers on this lonely country road in the dead of night?"

But cognizant of the fact that the other car could be filled with human-eating aliens, it was too dark to tell, I decided to terminate the conversation and vamoose on out of there.

Me: "Hey, thanks, I appreciate it."

Woman: "Good luck, and enjoy the rest of your evening."

After that I could only *sense* the other vehicle slowly moving away westbound on Brewer Road, away from Route 150. Despite the fact that their vehicle was within a few feet of mine, and my window was open, I do not recall hearing her tires rolling away against the road. Adrenaline overdose, perhaps?

As I turned to look in the direction of the departing vehicle I realized that it was navigating an absolutely pitch black road without its lights on! To this day I cannot imagine how anyone could navigate down that narrow road without headlights or driving lights and not crash. Impossible!

If your cabeza has ever come into sudden contact with a large solid object like a sneaky door or the back of your mother's disciplinary hand, then you know how I felt at this particular moment.

My head hurt from all the questions clamoring to get out. How did "she" know I was parked there? It was way too dark to see, my lights were out, and I'd been sitting there in the dark for several minutes prior to "her" appearance. Why did she stop? Who amongst us is in the habit of interrogating perfect strangers in the middle of the night on a dark lonely road? Certainly not any of my living friends!

Most importantly, how could she be so sure that "they would not be back?" Did she have a current hotline to the visitors or did they tell her their travel plans way back in 1965? Maybe she waited for them for the last forty years without satisfaction. And how did she drive that "car" down that narrow dark road without driving it into a tree or ditch? Too many unanswered questions. For me it was a mind expanding, unforgettable experience that left no doubt the Exeter UFO mystery was still alive and well in the former neighborhood of Norman Muscarello.

Regardless of the real answers to all these questions, one thing is evident. Local connection to the 1965 Norman Muscarello experience is still alive in Exeter, New Hampshire – never more so than in the shadow of the actual sighting, Pease Air Force Base.

Don't be fooled by the cheerful appearance of this Pease Air Force Base welcoming sign. In 1965 blue-suited nefarious sorts from this former Air Force base tried to scam local New Englanders into disbelieving their own eyes and were met with disastrous results.

Pease Air Force Base: A UFO Disinformation Disaster
No retelling of the Muscarello story is complete without a
visit to the former home of the government officials who tried to
obfuscate the truth, the whole truth and nothing but the truth and
insulted a generous portion of curious New Hampshire residents in
the process. We're talking about the US Air Force at Pease Air Force
Base located 12 miles northeast of Exeter.

In 1965 the US Air Force was still generously accepting UFO
reports from the public as part of its *Project Blue Book*. Back then the
trusting and naïve public thought that Blue Book was actually using
serious scientific methods to investigate and analyze sightings.
However, it is now established fact that Blue Book was nothing more
than a public relations cover whose only job was to explain every
sighting in prosaic terms regardless of the truth collected in their
reports. Their mantra was "deny, deny, deny" and this they tried to
do in the case of Exeter.

Faced with the impossible task of explaining dozens of 1965
local sightings, the US Air Force nonetheless gave it that old college
try. They assembled the skeptical witnesses in the field where
Muscarello had his second sighting and pointed their attention
towards Pease AFB twelve miles in the distance. Even a blind person
would have seen the epic fail that was about to transpire.

On cue the Pease AFB runway lights were turned off and on
several times by base personnel in an attempt to simulate the flashing
lights of the Exeter UFO. When not a single soul standing in the field
saw these runway lights flicker, because they could not be seen from
Norman's sighting location, the Air Force representatives were
hooted derisively into rapid retreat. Wisely they left before the good
citizens of Exeter and its environs treated them to a well-deserved
Revolutionary-era tar and feathering.

How desperate was the US Air Force to explain away the
Exeter sightings that they did not take the time to *test* their
explanation *before* they herded everyone into the field? When their
first explanation failed, they next claimed that the sightings were the
result of a "local nighttime lighted advertising sign that was regularly
towed behind a small airplane." Had they checked with the owner of
the sign, they would have discovered that the sign was not flown on

the nights of the major encounters, including those of Muscarello and the two police officers who were with him; desperate times required desperate measures indeed.

* * * *

Extraterrestrial interest in our nuclear capabilities is well known with many documented visits to nuclear power plants, nuclear weapon storage sights, nuclear research facilities and armed nuclear missile silos. In 1965 there was a generous supply of nuclear weaponry and nuclear material in and around Exeter.

Pease AFB was the home of America's 509th Bombardment group beginning in 1958 and continuing until 1991. This is the same nuclear capable fleet that was formerly housed at Walker Air Force Base in Roswell, New Mexico, near the famous location where the Air Force claimed to recover a "crashed disc" in 1947. Could our extraterrestrials observers have followed the nuclear 509th from Roswell to the Exeter area? There was also a US Navy nuclear powered submarine resting at the bottom of the ocean a few hundred miles outside of Exeter, complete with a nuclear reactor, where it remains to this day.

Pease AFB is now Portsmouth International Airport at Pease.

The former Pease Air Force Base is now home to the New Hampshire Air National Guard 157th Air Refueling Wing. The site hosts nearly 400 military personnel.

    If the extraterrestrial visitors needed an excuse to cruise Exeter for several months around September 1965, one need not look any further than the nuclear armed bomber fleet of the US Air Force that was located at Pease Air Force Base just a few miles away. Perhaps if the Air Force had told the curious public in Exeter that nukes were in their very backyard, the sons and daughters of the American Revolution could have figured out why they were seeing large glowing objects gliding low overhead in the dead of night. Instead they were left to ponder how easily the Air Force was fooled by lighted advertising signs and sleight of hand tricks with airport runway lights.

    As for Norman Muscarello, within weeks of his 1965 sighting he was in basic training with the Navy and was soon patrolling the rivers in Viet Nam where he did two tours. Muscarello was prematurely beamed off this planet in 2003 at age 55.

Chapter Epilogue

In the course of my 2008 visit and investigation in Exeter, I talked to literally dozens of the local citizenry and public servants, beyond those already mentioned, in my quest to locate new information for publication in this book. I talked to the police, the librarian, couples on the street, people in restaurants and retail stores. Many recalled reading the John Fuller book, some as a high school assignment. Few had thought about the Incident for decades.

In March 2015, I talked with Russell Fieldsend at length via phone to let him know I'd be in the area the following month to run the Boston Marathon, and if all went well would try to see him while I was there. Unfortunately the race was run in gusty headwinds up to 30 miles per hour, 43 degree temps, and a cold continuous rain. Needless to say I was too exhausted that evening to drive over to see him at the rest home where he now resides. Peace to you Russell and thanks for sharing your memories.

In 2010, Exeter, New Hampshire held its very first Exeter UFO Festival to commemorate and celebrate their story made famous by John Fuller in *Incident at Exeter*. Advertising for the 2015 rendition on their website posted the following invitation.

"Thanks to the Exeter Area Kiwanis Club, the Exeter UFO Festival will be back this year (2015). The festival has been held in downtown Exeter for the last five years, drawing UFO enthusiasts from across the country and many parts of the globe."

Key speakers scheduled were Stanton Friedman, Richard Dolan and my friend Jennifer Stein whom you'll read about later in this book.

Since this festival arrived in Exeter less than two years after I stirred the UFO pot with some of the essential witnesses in all the right locations – Exeter Inn, the Dining and Russell farms and the Police Station – is it possible that my actions caused the local citizenry to reconsider their UFO heritage and make it a positive rather than a negative? And what about that disembodied voice I encountered who spoke so emphatically on behalf of the intergalactic visitors?

The female disembodied voice I encountered that dark evening in September 2008, near Muscarello's UFO encounter site at the Dining/Russell farm location, predicted "they (the visitors) are not coming back". After some careful UFO-database information extraction and analysis by the author I'm here to report that I disagree.

In the years since the *Incident at Exeter* there have been just over 200 UFO reports filed with the National UFO Report Center for Exeter and its surrounding communities within a reasonable 10 mile radius. All shapes: diamond, triangle, disk, oval, sphere, teardrop, lights; all observation times: 6 seconds to one hour; by people from all walks of life: military and commercial pilots, white, blue and no-collar occupations; have been reported right up to the present day in September 2015.

As I write my final words on Exeter for this book I can't help but ponder the mystery that was my encounter with the disembodied female voice. When she spoke about the Exeter cosmic visitors by saying "they're not coming back" I took that as a cue to "get out of Dodge!" What she may have actually been saying to me is backed up by hundreds of UFO reports from the area. And that is, "They're not coming back. They don't have to 'come back' because they never left."

As of November 2015, Stephen Smith and Arthur Russell are both alive and doing well. Steve said that "all the helpful witnesses have damped off or were previously interviewed". A long phone conversation and correspondences with Steve confirmed this. Steve still insists on having limited first-hand knowledge of the incident. I still wonder about that. Peace.

Fortunately for the human race, the kind and often beleaguered citizens of Exeter were not the only people to experience multiple visits from extraterrestrials. Holding no favorites, intergalactic travelers visited our English cousins on the other side of the pond in December 1980, making an indelible impact on witnesses and researchers for over 35 years.

Adventure 2
Rendlesham Forest and Beyond

"You won't need a GPS when Fate is driving." – Author

UFOs Everywhere in the UK! The 2012 London Summer Olympics, Rendlesham Forest and Avebury Henge

In the wee, frozen morning hours of 26 December 1980, Royal Air Force (RAF) Station Woodbridge was desperately hiding two dark secrets from the rest of the unsuspecting world: Cold War-era nuclear-armed jet fighters ready to attack Russia, and stealthy visitors from another galaxy.

Quietly nestled in Rendlesham Forest on the southeast coast of England, RAF Woodbridge was, at the time, home to the United States Air Force 81st Tactical Fighter Wing, the tip of the nuclear spear during the Cold War. Unfortunately for the Air Force, neither the tall, dense pines of adjacent Rendlesham Forest nor the hulking, bomb-resistant jet hangars at RAF Woodbridge could effectively cloak Earth's most destructive weapons from curious out-of-this-world visitors.

Adhereing to some unwritten, intergalactic planetary visitation code, curious cosmic visitors chose the darkest hours to land a 9-foot long by 6-foot high triangular craft within a few hundred feet of Woodbridge's East Gate, a 24 hour high security patrol outpost. Serious US Air Force patrolmen manning this station saw the craft's strange lights in the Forest and were soon heading out in hot pursuit to investigate, beginning one of the most extraordinary UFO incidents ever placed on the official military record.

By the time the excitement had settled down, dozens of US military had witnessed multiple spacecraft sending down beams of light at the feet of the troops on the edge of Rendlesham Forest and onto the nuclear weapons storage area. Some of those troops had actually touched a spacecraft. A senior leader narrated an audio recording of himself and his troops chasing the craft through the forest. And the whole event was eventually documented by an official letter written from the US Air Force to the British Ministry of Defence. This was Rendlesham Forest in December 1980.

I just had to see this place for myself! How could I possibly make this trip happen? Fate had the answer.

Bomb resistant hangars at Royal Air Force Woodbridge protected nuclear capable jet fighters of the US Air Force 81st Tactical Fighter Wing until 1993, four years after the fall of the Berlin Wall. The hangar contents and nearby weapons storage bins were radioactive beacon lights for our curious cosmic visitors.

An unscheduled career retirement came in late 2011 as a result of traffic wreck injuries (not my fault). I immediately planned to fulfill a longtime promise that I'd visit Rendlesham Forest and spend time walking in the footsteps of the military UFO experiencers, convincing myself that their encounters were real. Since London was hosting the 2012 Summer Olympics and was theoretically a miniscule two hour drive from Rendlesham Forest, a timely trip to the UK was a no-brainer.

There was only one small problem with this impromptu plan, an unanticipated, surprisingly-American English appetite for Olympic sports. Surprising because mention of the United Kingdom had not struck fear in the hearts of any Olympic Village, winter or summer, since the days of English ski jumper Eddie "The Eagle" Edwards whose demonstrated lack of skill was likely to kill himself or his competitors at the 1988 Winter Games where he finished dead last – twice!

The United Kingdom were not world beaters by any stretch of the imagination. As recently as the 1996 games, the UK won only one gold and finished ranked 36th in the medals count. So I'm figuring the UK national Olympic psyche is a bit too fragile to overwhelmingly support the games. Instead, I mused, the locals will probably opt for pints in the pub and the games on the telly.

This could have been the worst underestimation of the British since we invited The Beatles, The Rolling Stones, and other mop-haired English bands in the early 60's, who then totally dominated the American music scene for that decade. In total, The Brits issued an unprecedented 20 million requests for the 6 million seats at the 2012 Olympics. There was only one thing to do, keep calm, carry on, and book a flight to London!

The Halt Memo: A Rendlesham Forest Smoking Gun!

Prior to the 2014 publication of *Encounter in Rendlesham Forest*, created in close cooperation with two of the principal event experiencers, US Airmen Jim Penniston and John Burroughs, relevant information was mostly second-hand and often tainted by unscrupulous debunkers posing as legitimate researchers. Yes, I know, using the word unscrupulous to describe debunkers is redundant.

That said, what inoculates the Rendlesham event from the noisy negativists who attack legitimate UFO cases is a letter written by Woodbridge Air Station's deputy commander, Lt. Colonel Charles Halt, to the British Ministry of Defence. That letter, submitted two weeks after the incident, detailed Woodbridge's US Air Force security force two-day encounter with intergalactic visitors, an encounter personally experienced by Lt. Colonel Halt himself on day two. I retrieved a copy of Halt's letter from my trusty backpack as my plane went nose up for London, refreshing my memory with his remarkable and unprecedented military admission to a close encounter.

The "Halt Memo", as it has become to be known to Ufologists, describes Woodbridge's US security forces first observing at close range a glowing, metallic, triangular object, 3 meters long on each side and 2 meters in height. The object left distinct landing depressions in the frozen ground and high levels of radiation in the landing area. The memo continues to describe additional UFO activities that occurred 48 hours later, observed close-up by dozens of US Air Force personnel, including Halt!

According to Halt, while his team was in the forest, they saw a "red sun-like object that pulsed" which "broke into five separate white objects, then disappeared." A short time later they saw "three star-like objects" moving in "sharp angular movements" displaying "red, green and blue lights." One of the objects stayed in the sky for "two to three hours and beamed down a stream of light from time to time."

Pause for a moment to get your head around these historic, written statements by a senior US Air Force Officer. This is the same US Air Force that said the 1947 Roswell Crash was a weather balloon, effectively throwing one of their finest Intelligence Officers under the bus, Major Jesse Marcel, by saying he could not tell the difference between a common rubber weather balloon and a piece of exotic alien spacecraft.

Lt. Col. Halt, a senior officer, carefully constructed an official document shortly after the affair, clearly stating that the US Air Force was chasing UFOs through Rendlesham Forest! This act of military bravery and candor is unmatched in the annals of UFO history.

As we neared Heathrow Airport I thought how critically important the Halt memo is to legitimate UFO researchers. Although the memo and subsequent related events did not put an end to ridiculous debunker explanations for unexplainable close encounters and lights in the sky, it did provide the smoking gun which proved that US government agencies were still concerned about keeping a lid on the UFO reality.

Lovely Rendlesham Forest adjoins the former home of nuclear aircraft. It hosted uninvited intergalactic visitors late in December 1980.

Go for the Olympics, Stay for the UFOs & Crop Circles

Departing Heathrow for Paddington Station via the Express Train, I christened my arrival in London at my favorite pub, *The Swan*, located across the street from Hyde Park where it was widely rumored I could find some Olympic athletes relaxing after a hard day's work. I thought "It's London 2012, why not?"

Easy to find, difficult to photograph from the middle of busy Bayswater Road, *The Swan* is across the street from famous Hyde Park. It's been open on this location for centuries.

No Olympians did I find at The Swan, but there were Nordic-type Olympic fans in ancient native dress with gold-horned helmets and intricately designed plastic swords and shields. As they moved through the crowded establishment guzzling beer like an 8th century siege was imminent, buxom pub staff yelled, "There be Vikings about!" mostly in mock terror.

It was all in good fun, the pub staff apparently remembering that real Vikings only invaded Britain in 300-year intervals – that was 793 AD and 1066 for those of you who snoozed through your

European history classes. While Vikings weren't actually invading London in July, 2012, I was totally dazed and delighted to discover that UFOs were!

A young Nordic gymnast practices for the 2028 Summer Olympics at *The Swan* during the 2012 Summer Olympics in London.

A UFO story was actually headline news during London Olympic week in that bastion of conservative British reporting *The Daily Mail*. As reported in *The Mail*, on the evening of Friday, 27 July 2012, a metallic saucer-shaped object - classic bulge in the middle - slowly moved over the Olympic Stadium, at the very moment the Olympic opening ceremonies came to a close around 12:30 am in Stratford, east London.

Under the 30 July 2012 headline "Beam me up, sporty! UFO spotted among fireworks at Olympics opening ceremony" writer Nick Enoch posited several "rational" explanations like a photography blimp, a helicopter, and a hoax in addition to it actually being a spaceship.

While the sharp video footage available on their website had me definitely thinking "helicopter" because of what looks like a flashing warning signal on the craft, the still photos shown on the same page are not like a helicopter at all. In my opinion, the still photos are definitely the shape of a classic saucer. From the evidence available on the *Mail's* website I'd have to call this one "unidentified." Whether it's extraterrestrial or not is another question. Either way, it was a very clever ploy to overcome a drastic ticket shortage!

And like most UFOs seen at a distance at night, a 100% positive ID by a reputable witness is highly unlikely. Regardless, Nick Pope, the principal author of the aforementioned book *Encounter in Rendlesham Forest*, had predicted weeks before the Olympics "that mass summer events would be a prime time for crafts from other worlds to present themselves to mankind."

If a positive ID is ever made on the *Daily Mail's* Olympic Stadium UFO sighting, I'm going to give "clairvoyant" Nick a call and ask for his advice on some long-term stock investments. I'll even pay for his beer consumption while he's making his choices. From personal experience that could be an illuminating but potentially costly proposition.

Wembley Stadium: Mothership or UFO Magnet?

With UFOs reported over Olympic stadiums, I was desperate to find a ticket to a large UFO-attracting venue. I raced to Wembley Stadium to score a ducat to the US vs Japan, Women's Gold Medal Soccer game. When I arrived at Wembley I disappointedly found a relatively new, massive gleaming structure capable of seating 90,000 fans, not the legendary Wembley Stadium in my memory which hosted The Rolling Stones, Queen, Live Aid 1985, The FA Cup Finals, the 1948 Olympics, the 1996 World Cup final and an endless list of historically significant events.

That Wembley Stadium I was to learn was torn down in 2003 and rebuilt on the same spot, to open in 2007 as the mothership of all stadiums in the UK. Worse, the ticket office would not open for an hour. Drat.

Discouraged but undaunted, I walked completely around the stadium ground closely trailed by two underutilized security guards who eventually accepted the fact I was merely sensing the energy left behind from all those famous events in the old Wembley, and not a local hooligan casing out the joint for an illegal entry. The guards agreed that I couldn't possibly be a United Kingdom gate-crasher as that ilk could not bother with such a long surveillance walk under the "excruciating" 78 degree heat being experienced that afternoon.

While I mused that this singularly British mindset regarding warmer temperatures could easily explain the Brits less-than-stellar performance in previous summer Olympics, I started to hear the theme song from *Chariots of Fire* playing in my head. Or maybe it was just the sweltering heat playing tricks.

On game day I was not surprised in the least to find that my game ticket placed me immediately behind the exuberant families of the American women's soccer team. I would like to attribute this fantastic fortune to the fact that I had indeed collected good energy while circumnavigating the venue prior to my arrival at the ticket window, and the fact that I have a choir boy face. Or it could have been the presence of my own personal security force who, forgetting they actually had a real job to do,

Above: Wembley Stadium. Is it really a Mothership in disguise?
Below: Soccer fans showing off spelling skills. What, no Japanese?

followed me right to the ticket window while regaling me with stories of the English Premiere League games they'd attended at the New Wembley. The ticket attendant must have reasoned that anyone with his own British security force and a US passport was trustworthy enough to mingle with Team USA parents on game day. We'll never know, but I'm betting on the choir boy face.

My impromptu security force.

To my delight, a 2-1 US victory touched off a raucous celebration in the US parents' section where I was close enough to see the tears of joy streaming down friendly faces. At that moment my security force was nowhere to be found, presumably home watching *Monty Python* reruns. Absent, too, was the previously seen silver spacecraft that failed to make an appearance over Wembley Stadium on that glorious evening. No worries though, more strange celestial happenings were arriving.

Victorious US Team celebrates Gold Medal with parents in 2012.

Identified Flying Objects Over Hyde Park

The 2012 Summer Olympic Games closed on 12 August after a two week run with spectacular fireworks and more celestial surprises. For those of us who could not score tickets to the Closing Ceremonies, there was a fantastic consolation prize in the form of a massive concert in Hyde Park starring rock bands Blur, New Order and The Specials. Yeah, I never heard of any of these guys either, but tickets for the Closing Ceremonies were impossible to get and I just wanted to party with my English cousins one more time before leaving London.

What better way to do that than join them for an historic concert in legendary Hyde Park where the likes of The Beatles, The Rolling Stones, The Who, Eric Clapton and just about every famous English rocker had rocked the world at one time or another. Oh, did I mention the awesomely brilliant meteor shower in the skies directly overhead the concert stage that night?

Yep. 12 August was the peak of a fantastic Perseid meteor shower which made its presence known in generous spurts throughout the evening portion of the concert. At times the drunken crowd's reactive *oohs* and *aahs* could actually be heard above the ear-splitting riffs emanating from the stage.

Yes, I'm painfully aware, using drunken and crowd to describe a British rock concert is redundant. That said, I am absolutely positive if meteorite showers were on the government's debunking list like UFOs, the media would have provided cover stories of "twinkling stars" and "glowing weather balloons" to explain what 80,000+ clearly saw over Hyde Park.

The debunkers would then give us the old "multiple space junk reentry story", their pièce de résistance to another incredulous hot steaming dump of UFO disinformation. Fortunately, the meteorite shower was so spectacular at viewing sites around the world, and reported so widely, that the debunkers had no choice but to sit in their kennels and loudly bay at planet Venus, their favorite "scientific" UFO explanation.

Carefully note that everyone in this photo has at least one beer in hand, the guy in the middle has two! UFO skeptics eventually claimed that "spontaneously combusted beer flatulence" was seen over the evening concert stage, rather than the widely reported meteorite shower.

The Long and Winding Road to Rendlesham Forest

Now where were we? Oh yes, the extraterrestrial craft landing at Rendlesham Forest, witnessed by dozens of military personnel, that authorities tried desperately to cover up, going so far as to drug the witnesses prior to, during and after their debriefing. More on the time honored drug-induced interrogation methods of "friendly forces" later.

With the Olympics concluded and a few remaining brain cells intact, I wanted to get to Rendlesham in a hurry. And I would have done just that were it not for some Olympic-created shenanigans by the rental car agency that cost precious hours because they had moved locations after I made my reservation – the address in my hand was now bogus.

The result was a long, unscheduled and unproductive visit to a very sketchy, vacant building in London, miles removed from where the rental agency was actually now situated. This was the kind of place Jack the Ripper would easily have called home.

The kindness of a complete stranger with good cell reception rewarded me with a dodgy street corner pick-up by the highly embarrassed rental car representative. Not wanting to squander an opportunity to be compensated for the inconvenience, nor play the part of the classic ugly American, I laid it on rather thick at the rental desk and drove away for Rendlesham with a much deserved upgrade – or so I thought.

Exactly how I was going to get there I wasn't sure because something, concert beer perhaps, made me forget to recharge the GPS that I had recently upgraded with a UK map module. As soon as I turned it on, the GPS turned itself off with that all too familiar and mocking "you forgot to recharge me again" blip.

Did I mention that the in-car charger adapter of my "upgraded" car was broken? Was this Instant rental Car-ma, apparently meted out for the gentle counseling I provided the rental car agent for leaving me stranded hours earlier? Or are the Brits still a bit touchy about that silly 13 American Colonies thing? I was about to be pissed, and not in the British way of thinking.

The theoretical two hour commute from London clocked in at a crisp three hours-plus as I was still steaming at the rental car agency for their negligence. The previous evening's beer was only partially responsible for my problem.

Twelve miles west of Rendlesham I managed to find the Belstead Brook Hotel in the pouring rain which had besieged me during the entire drive from London. Heavily draped in the rapidly approaching darkness and thickening English fog, the 16th century Belstead could have starred in any Sherlock Holmes movie requiring a creepy manor house; replete with a perched predator that eyed every unsuspecting visitor hungrily. After dinner and a cold beer I'd forgotten about the rental car fiasco, but not about charging the GPS, and I fell asleep dreaming of chasing UFOs the next day through nearby Rendlesham Forest.

Belstead Hotel's pugnacious predator prepares to pounce.

First Encounter at Rendlesham Forest

The Belstead serves a gigantic breakfast which I devoured in short order then headed to Rendlesham Forest with a fully charged GPS unit and a newly purchased 200-page atlas of the UK; yeah, I caved. Arriving at the former Woodbridge Royal Air Station on the edge of Rendlesham Forest, I pulled into a fair sized gravel parking lot situated almost on top of the small access road leading to the now famous East Gate.

The proximity of this lot to the access road leads me to believe it was built long after the base closed to accommodate the UFO researchers and enthusiasts to keep them from parking on the narrow road that runs between the base and Rendlesham Forest. I also believe having a parking lot so close to the East Gate during its operational years would have been security risk and would not have been tolerated by the base occupants. It was time for a deep breath. I had made it to the famous Rendlesham Forest of UFO lore and I was anxious to investigate.

Seeing London the prior week draped in the splendor of the Olympic Games was a once-in-a-lifetime delicacy. So, too, were the Hyde Park concerts, new pub friends and events seen live. But now I stood on the threshold of one on the best documented, yet fully unexplained mysteries on planet Earth: the US Air Force's Encounter in Rendlesham Forest.

I knew there wasn't going to be a Rendlesham ET landing for me to witness that day but there was something special in the air; much like you experience the moment just before your favorite band hits that first concert note, ending a very long anticipation. The door to the Rendlesham Forest UFO mystery lay in front of me and I didn't walk through, I ran through! And Rendlesham did not disappoint my insatiable need for mystery.

Right from the get-go my suspicious nature was tweaked when I spotted a black car in the uncrowded parking lot occupied by a man dressed in a crisply ironed, expensive dark suit wearing dark government-like sunglasses. Could the mysterious Men in Black, who reportedly harass UFO witnesses and destroy evidence, be staking out Rendlesham Forest 30-plus years after the fact?

Some interesting evidence I saw that day makes me think the answer is a definite "maybe". But since I didn't come all this way to be intimidated by some pseudo-government suit in cheap sunglasses, I headed out of my car to the place where it all started on that cold winter morning in December 1980, the Woodbridge East Gate, located at 52°05'24.09"N, 1°25'36.67"E.

Access road to the famous Woodbridge Royal Air Station East Gate.

Right At East Gate

"Very dangerous. You go first." Sallah to Indiana Jones, *Raiders of the Lost Ark*

On 26 December 1980, three US Airmen, Jim Penniston, John Burroughs and Ed Cabansag came down the East Gate access road, turned right, and followed strange lights they saw into the woods. A fellow security patrolman manning the East Gate believed the lights they had seen were from a crashed aircraft fire. However, that assumption was short lived as the lights appeared to maneuver slowly through the trees and pulsed with multiple colors not normally associated with a crash event.

Left: East Gate guard house from which US Air Force Security was dispatched on 26 December 1980.   Right: UK Ministry of Defence markers surrounding the former Woodbridge Royal Air Station.

With airman Cabansag dutifully maintaining a radio communication chain within the search area, Burroughs and Penniston slowly penetrated into the woods until they came face to face with a nine-foot long, eight-foot high, red glowing, triangular object that had apparently landed. The cold, damp forest suddenly became eerily silent. Then things got strange.

The East Gate used by US troops to pursue UFOs in December 1980.

According to Jim Penniston who now stood right next to the object, the exterior of the craft looked glass-like and there was a static electricity feeling to the air as he examined some three-inch-high hieroglyph-type shapes etched on the side panel. John Burroughs, standing nearby, noted that everything seemed to slow down time-wise giving him the feeling that he was moving in slow motion. Penniston removed his notebook from his pocket and began to make drawings of the craft shape and of the "hieroglyphs" that ran down the side of the craft. Then things got *really* strange.

For reasons that he cannot explain to this day, Jim Penniston reached out and placed his hand over the largest glyph. When he did so he was engulfed in a brilliant white light and simultaneously lost his senses of sight and hearing.

After an undetermined amount of time, his sight returned and Penniston found himself still standing next to the craft which began to turn a vivid white color. Fearing an explosion, he and Burroughs retreated to a defensive position and watched as the craft maneuvered to tree top level then disappear in the blink of an eye.

"Speed Impossible" is the last note Penniston entered in his notebook that evening to describe the craft's sudden departure. Little did he suspect then that the next day he would enter the most important information his notebook had ever seen – The Binary Code.

Unbeknownst to Penniston at the time, the act of placing his hand on the craft's largest glyph created a "data connection" that was used to download a lengthy and significant message, a message which he kept secret from his many interrogators and the world at large for over thirty years.

Troubled by an endless string of 1's and 0's running through his mind's eye the day after this initial encounter, Penniston sat down and filled sixteen pages of his notebook with what turned out to be modern binary code; easily decipherable today by first year computer science students. After he finished writing that day, the code he had apparently downloaded from the craft disappeared from his memory. He closed his notebook and never mentioned the code during any of his nearly two dozen interrogations nor anywhere else. It was as if the message originators had explicitly instructed Penniston to hide the message from sinister types, who would do anything to keep it from public revelation, until the time was right.

While Penniston was transferring the code in his head into his ever-present notebook, the uninvited visitors he courageously welcomed to Rendlesham were apparently still hanging around the neighborhood, looking for additional human thumb drives perhaps. In the late evening of 27 December 1980, nearly 48 hours after the initial Penniston/Burroughs encounter, a young lieutenant interrupted Lt. Col. Halt at an awards dinner to tell him that "the UFO is back." (Lt. Col. Halt will be referred to as Col. Halt going forward, reflecting his post-event promotion.)

Col. Halt, the deputy base commander, was subsequently directed by the base commander, Colonel Ted Conrad, to immediately take a team out to the current sighting location and conduct an investigation. At that very moment Col. Halt was standing on the precipice of UFO history, only he wouldn't know it until hours later when his extraordinary investigation ended.

For reasons that are not revealed anywhere, including in *Encounter in Rendlesham Forest*, Halt and his team did not directly investigate the new series of lights in the forest. Instead they headed to the earlier Burroughs/Penniston encounter site to conduct a retroactive investigation with a Geiger counter and to retrieve soil and tree sap samples from affected areas.

At that site they found unusually high radiation readings in several areas including the deep ground indentions made by the craft in the frozen ground, the ground in the center of the landing area, and the nearby trees on the sides facing the landing area; all consistent with a radioactive source landing exactly where Burroughs and Penniston had previously documented. According to Penniston their sighting took place at the following coordinates: 52° 05' 10.65" N, 1° 27' 00.01" E.

Since GPS devices were not in use in 1980, Penniston and Burroughs used grid maps of Rendlesham Forest to report their whereabouts, and this information was available in the event reports for Halt and his team to use on their investigation two days later. While Halt and his team were in the middle of their investigation, they spotted a red light moving through the woods to their north.

Col. Halt had a Lanier voice recorder he used to document the team's progress and he judiciously used it to describe the moving light as "looking like a blinking eye." Halt and his team moved northerly along the eastern edge of the forest to follow the moving light, stopping at a point about 200 yards north of the Penniston/Burroughs site. The coordinates of their new location was 52° 05' 18.14 N, 1° 27' 00.06 E". Looking due east from this point one can see the farmhouse referenced in the many descriptions of the Rendlesham Forest event.

Upon reaching this new destination, Halt and company saw the mysterious red light hover in the open barren field now in front of them, its light reflecting off the nearby farmhouse windows.

Suddenly it burst into five separate sections of glowing brilliant white light that moved off into different directions.

Standing at the eastern edge of Rendlesham Forest viewing the house and farm where animals went crazy while UFOs were in the vicinity. The location of the second night's sighting by Col. Halt and his team is a few hundred feet north of the Penniston/Burroughs initial encounter site two days earlier. Location: 52° 05' 18.14 N, 1° 27' 00.06 E

The team continued to see large, moving, lighted objects in the sky for the next four hours or so. Some of these objects projected beams of light right down to the ground, at one point virtually at the feet of the awestruck military investigation team. When they reached their furthest point east at around 0400 hours, they turned their attention toward Woodbridge Base to discover that one of the unknowns was now directly over the base and projecting a beam of light into the nuclear weapons storage area.

Throughout the otherworldly five-hour investigation by Col. Halt and his military team, he kept a running commentary of the events unfolding in front of them on his Lanier voice recorder. These tape recordings later proved to be immutable evidence that something extraordinary had indeed transpired in Rendlesham Forest in December 1980, with dozens of witnesses.

In the immediate days after the UFO encounters, word of the events leaked into the base population despite the fact that all known witnesses were sworn to secrecy. Many of the unlucky participants were subjected to multiple interrogations by agencies both known and unknown to them – all were "friendly forces."

Interrogation subjects have claimed that the nefarious interrogators used a variety of drugs to elicit information and to obfuscate the memories of the participants as part of the cover-up of the events in Rendlesham Forest. Despite over a dozen different intense interrogations, Jim Penniston was able to hang on to not only the unbelievable memories of the widely witnessed events but to his precious personal notebook which held the most important secret of the entire bizarre episode – The Binary Code.

It was only through pure chance that Penniston would eventually reveal the existence of his notebook's coded message to John Burroughs, his partner the night of the incident. He revealed it during the filming of a documentary interview. The 16-page sequence of 1's and 0's he had recorded were eventually given to a binary code expert whose straightforward translation revealed that the owners of the triangular craft that Penniston touched were here for the purpose of "The Exploration of Humanity."

Also included in the message were the geographic coordinates for several well-known and compelling earthly locations including the Great Pyramids of Giza, the Nazca Lines in Peru, a sacred temple in China, and a site in Sedona, Arizona, well known for its cosmic vortices. Equally astounding, the message states that the craft is a time traveler from the year 8100!

The pièce de résistance, if there can be such a thing for this event, is the fact that this extraordinary message lay dormant in the pages of Penniston's notebook for three decades simply because he had no idea that the stream of 1's and 0's he had recorded in his notebook had any meaning; he wasn't a computer geek and to him it looked like nothing more than a random, meaningless string of unrelated numbers.

As a certified computer geek many times over, I would have immediately recognized the 1's and 0's for what they were – a message from the cosmos. However, all things considered, like his drug-based interrogations, his lifetime of medical maladies, and his constant hassle from the government, I'm happy it was Penniston and not I who was chosen by the visitors to "take one for the team."

*   *   *

A No Frills Binary Code Primer

1. Computer Binary Code uses precise groups of 1's and 0's to represent printable alphanumeric characters and more
2. Binary Code is also used for control characters like a "space" between words in a sentence.
3. Each printable or control character is represented by a predetermined combination of eight, 1's and 0's.
4. When you type *I love you* the computer stores the following sequence of grouped 1's and 0's, i.e. binary code.

Binary Code	Character Represented
01001001	I
00100000	space
01101100	l
01101111	o
01110110	v
01100101	e
00100000	space
01111001	y
01101111	o
01110101	u

Strange Personal Encounters in Rendlesham Forest

Earlier in the day I'd spent considerable time researching around the East Gate, the base perimeter, and the access road before heading east into the forest. Just prior I observed that the suspected Man in Black was still in his car and I would eventually note that he would spend about four hours silently sitting there next to the East Gate access road. What could be so interesting?

I *so* wanted to sneak up on him the way Elmer Fudd does rabbits, then rap on his window to scare him into a reaction. But I decided that it was not a good day to get shot in the head or be subjected to a drug-fueled interrogation, so I reread my forest map and left the parking lot minus any life-threatening injuries.

As I headed into the same pine forest that Burroughs and Penniston had entered so long ago in December 1980, I noticed there was a very suspicious van parked on the narrow forest road about 75 feet south of the East Gate access road. With the obvious availability of the car park so close, and the forest road so narrow, it defies simple logic as to why the van was parked on the grassy roadside nearly the entire day.

Perhaps it was an insidious trap for anyone curious enough to get too close. The inquisitor would be snatched inside through the sliding side door by a team of agents dressed in black combat fatigues and full face masks. The abductee would get an unscheduled ether nap and would require a Liam Neeson rescue. Or worse yet, the inquisitive snooper would be rewarded with a near-lethal whiff of a stale, sunbaked child's diaper. In either case, it was a seemingly perilous situation I did not want to experience in the middle of Rendlesham on that unusually warm summer afternoon.

Eventually, though, I did muster the pluck to cautiously approach the vehicle and have a quick peek inside, but did not see any obvious surveillance equipment, kidnappers, or diapers. Although there was no appearance of danger that doesn't mean it was totally absent. "Just because I'm paranoid doesn't mean nobody is watching", I always say.

In my loops though the forest that day with some stops back at my car for snacks, I did not see any human activity at the van. I silently ventured it was either owned by an infamous intelligence agency or just some inebriated English chap with extremely poor driving habits. With 100,000 official annual busts for drink driving in the UK, that was my initial leading theory.

Later researching the van's license plate number I did discover that the car was registered in Peterborough, Cambridgeshire, over a two hour drive from Rendlesham - and "surprise" - home of RAF Molesworth, a base run by the US and crawling with intelligence assets. Yikes! Why would Intel assets still be interested in Rendlesham after all these years?

Based on this new information I offer my sincerest apologies to every inebriated driver in the UK with extremely poor driving habits. You are hereby fully exonerated for the Rendlesham parking infraction. On the other hand, it would appear that the intelligence agency employees are in desperate need of some remedial training on UK parking regulations.

The mystery van of Rendlesham Forest parked off-road. Was it owned by careless intelligence assets or underachieving student drivers?

In the immediate area of the mystery van I met several like-minded individuals (not the van owners, I checked) who were also nosing around Rendlesham, but none more interesting than the extended family pictured below. The adults were all UFO "enthusiasts" and were sharing their keen paranormal interests with their young, impressionable children.

Rendlesham UFO enthusiasts on Woodbridge's East Gate access road.

Nothing says "family bonding" quite like a visit to *the* creepy forest where extraterrestrial visitors outflanked the brightest minds of the US military, who were safekeeping nuclear weapons, in a game of hide-and-seek, and in the process provided many of those same military witnesses with documented doses of "missing time". And let's not forget the after-the-fact, involuntary, drug-induced interrogations by friendly forces. Maybe later we'll watch *Jack the Ripper*. Sweet dreams kids!

After endlessly regaling these new found friends with my in-depth knowledge of the Rendlesham episode they enthusiastically gave me the internationally recognized, "Arthur Fonzarelli, thumbs-up seal of approval."

The *really* scary part was the little blond girl who stuck her thumb up, then stared at it for the next 30 seconds, as if it was going to turn into a dragon or a fairy. If I had to pick someone from this group that had already seen cosmic visitors and had subsequently stared into a *Men in Black* "clicky-flashy neuralizer", she's my hands-down choice. I probably should have asked *her* for help on the Forest Service code-challenge, a daunting task open to all Rendlesham visitors.

If you visit Rendlesham Forest be prepared for the Forest Service's (FS) contribution to the Rendlesham story in the form of "The UFO Trail". The UFO Trail theoretically follows the paths of the Rendlesham UFO witnesses to the trails and sites where the actual events occurred. According to the FS website, each trail marker contains a symbol that should be combined with many other symbols found on the trail markers to create a coded message. Good luck with this one.

After observation and analysis, I firmly believe that there is no coded message decipherable from the symbols found on The UFO Trail, and that this task is yet another harmless but cruel joke on the UFO community to distract them from doing real research. If you decide to tackle this mental gymnastics exercise might I suggest taking along a certified genius from Mensa to give your team a fighting chance.

Based on my earnest research I found the accuracy of the FS markers I encountered a hit and miss proposition, but they do provide thought-provoking conversation starters and an excellent chance to explore the dense woods without getting hopelessly lost; not that I would know anything about that getting lost thing.

While collecting the clues from The UFO Trail signposts I began to suspect that the coded message had something to do with documented alien interest in the female anatomy and hybridization. What the message is exactly I'm not quite sure.

Typical signs discovered along the Rendlesham Forest UFO Trail.

After seeing the "parking lot" Man in Black, the suspicious van, the "thumb girl", and Disney-like Forest Service alien signs, actually looking for the two encounter sites in the forest was almost anti-climactic. Based on information available today, I am 100% convinced that I found the Halt encounter site, as reflected in the photo with the field and farmhouse shown previously. And now knowing where the Burroughs/Penniston site is located, I am convinced I walked within several yards of it but did not know it at the time.

This failure would have been disappointing if I had a Geiger counter and missed a good chance to verify the higher than normal radiation readings at the Burroughs/Penniston site as reported in the Halt Memo. But seeing as how I was already outsmarted by my own GPS and the rental car guy to boot, it's a good thing I wasn't handling expensive and delicate equipment used to measure nuclear radiological energy.

Left: Reputed UFO landing site in Rendlesham Forest. Those in the know disagree with the Forest Service's geography. Right: Typical view of Rendlesham Forest as seen from the road which divides the forest from the former Woodbridge Royal Air Station.

After I had thoroughly satisfied my long running curiosity with a number of loops through the relevant part of the forest, it was still a long way from nightfall when I had planned to spend a few spooky flashlight-filled hours on The UFO Trail. Retreating to nearby Woodbridge Golf Club to kill some time, I introduced myself to the Pro Shop personnel who were delighted to host a player who said, fibbed actually, that he travelled over 4,000 miles just to play their delightful, heathland course.

I played the course until it was nearly dark along with the rest of the hardcore golfers, and actually survived the 4th hole which serves as a convenient human target practice zone for players teeing off on the 17th hole. Later, I ate a couple of granola bars and drove back in the dark to the Woodbridge access road parking lot, nervously anticipating I would not be alone when I arrived. I was understandably concerned about the Man in Black.

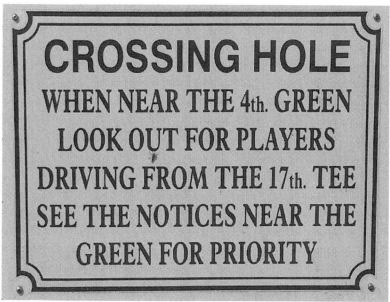

Woodbridge Golf Club, a lovely site complicated by occasional friendly crossfire on the 4th hole. It's also the 75th ranked course in England.

*   *   *   *

I do not understand why gravel surfaces make so much more noise in the dark of night than they do in the daytime but such was seemingly the case when I re-parked my car near the East Gate access road. Remarkably the Men in Black car was missing along with the mystery van that had been parked illegally on the berm of the forest road for most of the day.

Not unexpected was the extreme level of darkness in the middle of the forest through which I would attempt a flashlight-led

69

expedition to simulate the experience of Burroughs, Penniston, Halt and the rest of the witnesses – hopefully minus the extraterrestrial laser beams, "missing time", blinding lights and binary code telepathic download drama.

Having walked the trails in the daytime and pre-plotted a course for the evening, I cautiously proceeded to the Halt site at the far eastern end of the forest, via a very wide trail, where the farmhouse lights would twinkle through a bit of mist. Like the aforementioned gravel parking lots, the pine needle and twig laden trails seemed to crunch unexpectedly loud beneath my feet as I imagined Little Red Riding Hood wolves emerging from the dark to have their daily meal.

Was I concerned? You betcha! It's due to the substantial amount of gripping nervous tension that continuously builds in the chest and brain of the lone person proceeding into the dark, UFO-infested forest. I know this from personal experience.

The heightening volume of the sound from underfoot had me raising several survival questions. Is there any possibility I would encounter aliens? How about ill-tempered humans? Men in Black or wild animals? The owners of the illegally parked van or, more threatening, strange little girls staring at their thumbs?

It wasn't until weeks later that I learned the wolf, England's leading predator, was extinguished 300 years ago and the most ferocious predators in that forest were rabbits, albeit large, aggressive ones I understand. The remainder of the aforementioned menacing possibilities was still in play as I cautiously followed the path, dimly lit by my underpowered, hand-cranked "torch" – light output equal to two matchsticks.

After a cautious and lengthy tension-filled commute through the pitch black forest, I stood there on a pleasant summer evening overlooking the same silent field where cosmic craft had landed and had greatly disturbed veteran military men decades ago. At that moment I silently and simultaneously wished for a UFO sighting of my own *and* a safe journey back to my car on the other side of the forest, plainly incompatible goals.

One thing is certain. While standing alone in the dark, armed only with a small rechargeable flashlight at the site of an incredible

UFO encounter where ominous objects beamed down lights on the witnesses, I decided with indefensible logic that I was infinitely safer standing there than the 4th hole at nearby Woodbridge Golf Club. Although it is true that one can usually see a gigantic glowing UFO approaching, the same cannot be said of an errant golf ball coming at you around 100 miles per hour.

The reality is, both objects will probably "get you" if you are standing in the wrong spot.

While I meditated in the quiet blackness of the Halt UFO encounter site, I examined one of the more reasonable theories offered by the debunkers to explain lights in the woods; that a local lighthouse in Orfordness, several miles east of Woodbridge, may have contributed to the lights seen in the forest and fields.

Based on my personal nighttime observations in Rendlesham Forest, the lighthouse categorically cannot explain any of the key witness event descriptions. The lighthouse would not have been in the correct relative geographic location to explain Halt's sighting when he was standing at the Burroughs/Penniston site and became aware of the "blinking eye" his team spotted. Halt claims to be looking nearly due north, "120 degrees" away from his current location when he saw the moving lights, yet the lighthouse was to his east at that time.

Further, an evening observation I made from the East Gate revealed that the lighthouse was not visible at all from that location so those guards could not have been fooled by a lighthouse as argued by "skeptics". Most significantly, in their extraordinary encounter, Burroughs and Penniston said they saw a landed craft and Penniston said he "touched a landed craft." His subsequent drawing of said craft did not resemble a lighthouse in any way shape or form, something the debunkers have always refused to acknowledge - no surprise there.

Based upon my on-site, first person assessment it's safe to say that the lights from the Orfordness lighthouse, which by design never pointed towards Woodbridge, could not contribute to the lights and events described by Halt, Penniston, Burroughs and others. And to the debunkers, if you were not there on the nights that these folks had their encounters - then please, shut the hell up! You were not there and therefore your baseless opinions do not matter in any Rendlesham discussion. Amen.

The long quiet walk back to the car was uneventful except in my overly stimulated imagination where I wondered exactly what I would do should the suspicious van or the Men in Black car be present once again upon my return. Spookier yet would be the presence of someone standing in front of my car with a flashlight illuminating their face as they stared at their thumb. I needed a cold beer in the worst way.

Fortunately the parking lot was empty except for my vehicle which was looking more and more like a life raft as I nervously searched for the keys to unlock it. Almost safe inside I could not ignore the crunching gravel underneath my feet, which I knew was quickly alerting enemies near and far of my unprotected presence. I also could not ignore the creepy feeling that I was being closely watched by agents from Molesworth Royal Air Station, presumably hiding nearby. Again, just because I'm paranoid doesn't mean nobody is watching!

The UK UFO adventure *should* have ended once I got back to the Belstead Brook Hotel that night, snuck past the hungry hawk loitering on the chimney, wrote some notes and settled back into my bed. That was the way I was planning it anyway, with the rest of the trip to be consumed with golf at several Royal courses and time spent doing the Beatles thing in Liverpool for a few days. Those early plans thankfully changed for the better when I decided to visit Avebury Henge, the world's largest prehistoric stone circle.

Getting Stoned by Avebury Henge Crop Circles

Avebury Henge *is* the world's largest prehistoric stone circle. Located only 24 miles from Stonehenge, Avebury Henge is a virtual opposite to its enormously famous sibling where visitors are only allowed to touch the megalithic stones but once a year on the Summer Solstice.

Not so at Avebury Henge. It is 16 times larger than Stonehenge and actually surrounds a small village, but lacks the sexy horizontal lintel stones of its famous sibling. Displaying not a hint of Stonehenge's crusty arrogance, the kind folks of Avebury Henge say "You may fondle our stones all day if you so desire." I'm relieved to report that I did not find this unofficial town motto on any of the souvenirs in the gift shop.

The author enjoyed Avebury Henge where everyone hugs their stones.

While I was taking embarrassing selfies hugging the huge Avebury stones or interrupting other visitors to take my picture, I was informed by one of my more astute fellow tourists that there was a crop circle in the adjacent field to the village, just on the other side

73

of a farmer's fence. As has been widely reported, crop circles are the likely product of an extraterrestrial presence possibly using directed energy "drawing tools." Or, as Patty Greer the crop circle lady has suggested, crop circles could be created by some unknown energy emitted directly by the planet Earth.

But just my luck, I didn't bring a Geiger counter which I could have used to test the circle for radiation and possibly validate whether it was authentic or hoaxed. What the heck, I had never been in a crop circle before – and seriously - just how much radiation could stalks of crushed grain retain anyway? And couldn't we all use a third arm to firmly hold those frustrating cocktail party hors d'oeuvre plates?

Using urban survival skills developed and perfected while growing up in the mean streets of Detroit, I easily penetrated the farmer's fence without pulling a hamstring or ripping a gaping hole in my pants. I immediately discovered that crop circles in the UK are actually a "cash crop" so to speak. After reading the farmer's plea for donations at the entry to his crop circle field I had to wonder which came first, the farmer's convenient collection box or the seemingly authentic crop circle.

Experienced crop circle researchers might have been able to answer my suspicions of authenticity by measuring radiation in and out of the circle and examining the involved plants at a cellular level. Many crop circle plants exhibit significantly higher radiation levels within the crop circle than outside of it. And Biophysicists, like the late Dr. C.W. Leavengood, have proven cellular level plant changes *do* occur in authenticated crop circles.

Crop circle adjacent to Avebury Henge and convenient collection box.

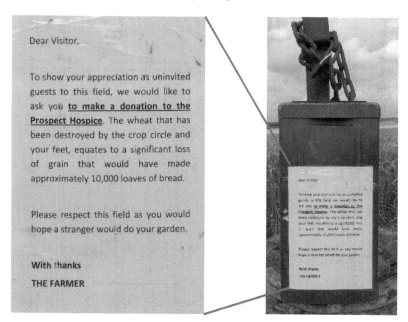

Dear Visitor,

To show your appreciation as uninvited guests to this field, we would like to ask you **to make a donation to the Prospect Hospice**. The wheat that has been destroyed by the crop circle and your feet, equates to a significant loss of grain that would have made approximately 10,000 loaves of bread.

Please respect this field as you would hope a stranger would do your garden.

With thanks

THE FARMER

For a moment I considered using a sandwich bag to collect some evidence from the circle and return it to the States with me for evaluation by some reputable researchers and their laboratories. But then, while mindlessly marveling in the middle of the crop circle with a dozen "hippy trippy" people who were apparently flashing back to their Woodstock days, I imagined the following possible conversation with our eagle-eyed US government customs agents.

US Customs: "Welcome back to the USA. Do you have anything to declare?"

Author: "No."

US Customs: "Are you sure?"

Author: "Well, I have this sandwich bag filled with wheat stalks that are probably radioactive because they were crushed by an extraterrestrial spacecraft which landed in Avebury. As you can see, the exposed stalks produced five times the seed of the control samples I collected away from the site and will produce offspring exhibiting the same miraculous genetic mutation for eternity; possibly changing the world's agriculture forever."

US Customs: "Uh huh. You may proceed. You're good to go!"

Author: "Have you ever heard of Rendlesham Forest and the night that cosmic visitors came to Woodbridge Royal Air Station to count our secret nuclear weapons?"

US Customs: "Code Red, everybody! Code Red! Someone contact Homeland!! Don't move mister!!!"

Chapter Epilogue

"It ain't over till it's over." New York Yankees baseball legend, Yogi Berra

Only a fool would try to deny that United States Air Force personnel encountered a UFO in Rendlesham Forest in December 1980. There are way too many highly qualified, cooperative witness testimonies and too much evidence produced for anyone to arrive at any other reasonable conclusion.

Despite two fact filled, first person, full length books published by the witnesses, the previously mentioned Pope/Penniston/Burroughs *Encounter in Rendlesham Forest*, and *Left at East Gate* by Larry Warren and Peter Robbins, along with dozens of TV shows and documentaries, I still had many questions when I returned from Rendlesham. To get answers I was privileged to have personal discussions with key witness and *Rendlesham* author John Burroughs, *Rendlesham* author Nick Pope, and researcher Linda Moulton Howe. I also had email exchanges with key witness and *Rendlesham* author Jim Penniston.

In addition to the above one-on-one dialogues with the witnesses and researchers, I also attended Rendlesham presentations by Nick Pope, a total of 4 hours at the 2014 Contact In The Desert (CITD), and by Linda Howe, one hour at the 2015 CITD, and was able to ask the speakers questions in those public forums. What follows are some of the interesting questions and answers from those exchanges. After all these years it's interesting to note what we still don't know about the UFO event in Rendlesham Forest. New revelations seem to appear weekly at conferences and on the web.

What interesting observations are on the extra minutes or hours of the unreleased Halt Tapes? After all, only 18 minutes have been released and Col. Halt was out there for over four hours.

Col. Charles Halt used a handheld voice recorder to document his team's investigation and encounter in Rendlesham over a four hour period as they chased and were being chased by glowing objects in the forest. To date, only eighteen minutes or so of those tapes have been released. There has to be a massive amount of intriguing and revealing information on those tapes that are pure gold to UFO researchers. So what is the status of those tapes?

In a 10 December 2014, *Dark Matters* podcast interview with Alejandro Rojas, Col. Halt claims that he only had one tape with him that night and all the material on that tape was released by a Col. Sam Morgan. But if you examine the answers provided to me by the individuals below, it would appear as if there is more taped material that Col. Halt has not released.

In that fascinating podcast interview where Col. Halt was joined by Rendlesham witness John Burroughs, he expressed some extraordinarily ominous views regarding government UFO cover-ups and John's fight to obtain rightfully earned medical attention (also discussed in another question below). Their relevant discourse is followed by additional comments on the tape status.

Halt: "What I've been trying to tell you for a long time, John, the tree you're barking up doesn't have the answers. I can't tell you on the air, but I can (muffled) tell you"

Burroughs: "Well, what tree am I barking up?"

Halt: "You keep saying the government's doing this, not doing that, and won't release this. It's something beyond what you're familiar with and I'm familiar with that's keeping things the way they are. Read between the lines."

Quickly "reading between the lines" was host Rojas who asked Halt the following question:
Rojas: "You alluded that there's something *above* the government?"

Halt: responded "That's my personal opinion. The politicians come, the politicians go".

Until I heard Col. Halt say there is a secret government controlling the UFO story, I had never before heard a senior military officer make that dark of a conspiracy claim. That's very scary stuff, indeed.

*   *   *   *

Nick Pope and the author at Joshua Tree, CA, May 2014.

Nick Pope declined comment on the Halt tape and graciously offered to provide me with Col. Halt's email address, if given permission by Col. Halt to do so, in order for me to ask Halt directly about unreleased taped evidence. The acquisition of Col. Halt's email is still a work in progress.

Jim Penniston claimed the tapes were "Halt's to do with as he pleases" and thought an upcoming presentation in Woodbridge by Halt in a July 2015 might provide more taped information. That conjecture has not yet been verified.

When I queried Linda Moulton Howe at her CITD 2015 lecture on Rendlesham she speculated that Col. Halt "might be preparing a book on his own and would likely include additional segments from the tapes in his book." Again, this speculation could not be verified.

So there you have it. Witnesses and researchers close to Col. Halt consistently indicating there is more tape to be revealed. However, Col. Halt is on record saying that he has published all of the single tape's contents. Could this be a case similar to the Rendlesham "binary code" where we'll have to wait another 30 years to find out about additional available evidence? I believe that if there is additional taped evidence on Col. Halt's tape, its way past time to make that evidence available to everyone. Or is Halt hesitant or unable to do so because of the scary "secret government" that Halt mentioned on the radio show?

How is it possible that The Binary Code stayed hidden for 30 years?!

This is an especially puzzling question since Jim Penniston, whose notebook held The Binary Code, was hypnotically regressed in 1994 and the code's existence was most certainly exposed during those sessions. The Eureka moment did not arrive until sixteen years later, 2010, when someone put 2 and 2 together after Jim revealed he had recorded the code in his notebook.

According to a Penniston email, neither he nor anyone else made a connection between the phrase "binary code" he spoke under hypnosis in 1994 and the information he recorded in his notebook. The reason this occurred will only make you shake your head and wonder at who was analyzing his regression tapes.

Jim did not know that the string of 1's and 0's he recorded in his notebook were called "binary code." More importantly, no one but Jim knew that the "binary code" he referred to in his hypnotic regression was actually recorded in his notebook. Further, he did not review his regression tapes and the hypnotist apparently did not emphasize that part of the hypnosis results during review sessions because he was also clueless.

Since Jim did not know what he had written in his book was binary code, anyone referring to his hypnosis usage of binary code, and asking Jim about it, would probably have been told "I don't know what you're talking about."

It wasn't until he was taping a documentary in 2010 that he initiated a conversation with his former Rendlesham security police force member, John Burroughs, and let John look at his notebook. In the process of that conversation, John identified the writing in Penniston's notebook as binary code - and "the rest is history" as they say.

In the same *Dark Matters* podcast mentioned previously, Col. Halt and John Burroughs speculated that Penniston's Binary Code may have come from a drug-induced indoctrination at the hands of friendly agents rather than a download from the craft he touched. This theory was floated on the broadcast despite the fact that Penniston insists he received the binary code while his hand was in contact with the landed craft in Rendlesham Forest.

Are the hypnotic regression tapes of Burroughs and Penniston available to researchers?

According to Jim Penniston he gave his regression tapes to Linda Moulton Howe who wrote a book about them. All efforts to email contact Linda on this subject, and several others topics, including one she personally asked me to write her about, have yet to be answered. She is a very busy person I presume.

If the US government is in denial about the Rendlesham Forest incident and has classified the medical records of John Burroughs and Jim Penniston, how will either of them ever get rightfully compensated for their Rendlesham-induced medical problems?

This question was answered publicly in a presentation given by John Burroughs at the 2015 IUFOC in Fountain Hills, Arizona. Although I had planned to attend his presentation I had to defer in order to witness a hypnotic regression being conducted at the exact same time as John's talk. Fortunately I was able to meet with John later that evening and discuss the situation with him at length.

John briefly went through a history of his case starting with the fact that the US Government claimed he was not in the Air Force in 1980, the year he claims he was injured. This ridiculous excuse was tendered despite the fact that he was holding official records in his hands proving quite the contrary! At the same time, the government refused to release his medical records to him, claiming they were classified. Unbelievable!

With the help of his lawyer, Pat Frascogna, and U.S. Senator John McCain's office, his service records were eventually corrected. Then he got his hands on a formerly classified Ministry of Defence Intelligence document that showed a correlation of medical injuries to exposure of radiation-bearing Unidentified Aerial Phenomena (UAP), like the one he encountered in Rendlesham Forest. After years of legal action John has received his full medical disability from the Veteran's Administration when they finally recognized the link between his illness and the UFO, or UAP, he encountered in Rendlesham.

Quoting from their press release at the 2015 IUFOC, John and his lawyer now claim their victory represents the "U.S. government's de facto acknowledgement of the existence of UFOs."

It will now be interesting to see how many more Rendlesham military witnesses come forward for medical disability as a result of the favorable judgment John has recently received. Hopefully they will add their stories to the best documented UFO case available, Rendlesham Forest.

The author and John Burroughs pose following their discussion at the 2015 IUFOC in Fountain Hills, Arizona.

Adventure 3
A Day with Travis Walton

Voices in My Head

2,000 Light Years From Home – Song by The Rolling Stones

There are rock stars and then there are Rock Stars, every generation has them. Frank Sinatra, Elvis Presley, The Rolling Stones, The Beatles, Michael Jackson, Aerosmith, AC/DC, Eminem. You know who they are.

In the decidedly eclectic world of Ufology Travis Walton is a Rock Star. Unlike the hall of famers listed above, Travis didn't have to master his trade to gain fame, he just needed to be in the wrong place at the wrong time; hard to believe but painfully true.

In November of 1975, Travis Walton stepped out of a beat up pickup truck on the edge of the Apache-Sitgreaves National Forest and into intergalactic history. His incredible story of alien abduction and unlikely return is the subject of books, movies, and endless documentaries.

I had the unique privilege of spending an entire afternoon with Travis taking photos and conducting a mini research project at the very site of his "encounter", a few miles outside of Heber, Arizona; just me and him. This is our story.

Gearing up for the 24th Annual International UFO Congress in Fountain Hills, Arizona, in February 2015, I was packing the usual stuff – clothes, toiletries, marathon training gear, and protein powder. Unannounced, my usually annoying inner voice woke up and said "pack your compass". I have a compass; a gift from an old friend that is a materially exact reproduction of Thomas Jefferson's and was only available from the Smithsonian Institute gift shop. It holds an honored place in my home office and has not moved off the curio shelf for over 20 years. The voice in my head said to pack the compass and I obliged.

I have a 35mm Canon 20D professional camera and lenses which would not be needed on this trip as my cell phone camera would suffice for the obligatory UFO book-author/fan selfies. The voices said louder "Pack your camera and gear." I obliged.

The voices in my head then said "After the conference you are going to the site of the Travis Walton encounter and will shoot photos." Whoa! The Travis Walton site is very near top secret, now known to but a few and those few are virtually sworn to secrecy.

Although I had researched the location of the Walton site for a year and knew I could get geographically close, maybe a couple hundred feet, I would never know exactly how close. But I was ready to oblige my inner voice and prepared for a trip to higher elevations. Fate can *sometimes* be a wonderful thing.

We-Ko-Pa Resort and Casino near Fountain Hills, Arizona, hosted several UFO Congresses. A two hour drive from the Apache-Sitgreaves National Forest, location of the Travis Walton abduction, it was my launching pad to his historically significant UFO site near Heber, AZ.

The Beginning of the Travis Walton Saga

On Wednesday, 5 November 1975, Travis Walton was a member of a seven man tree-cutting crew working the entire day in the Apache-Sitgreaves National Forest, several miles south of Heber, Arizona. His crewmates consisted of Allen Dalis, Dwayne Smith, John Goulette, Kenneth Peterson, Mike Rogers, and Steve Pierce. The crew was working on a US Forest Service contract known as the Turkey Springs tree-thinning contract owned by the crew foreman, Mike Rogers.

At 6 pm, 15 minutes after sunset, the tired crew shut down their chain saws and began packing up their gear into their vintage 1965 International Harvester. By 6:10 pm the crew and their gear were all packed up and heading slowly over bumpy roads to the Mogollon Rim Road when they spotted an exceptionally strange light coming through the trees.

It was 1975 and very few people knew about the insidious dangers that are strange lights seen on dark deserted forest roads; the Rendlesham Forest incident with its strange lights and similar consequences was still five years away. Because "Ray's UFO Avoidance Rules" were not available back in 1975 I'm giving Travis and his coworkers the benefit of the doubt. However, history does show that Travis and his fellow loggers made several epically bad decisions in a very short period of time once they saw the unusual lights in the woods.

Ignoring Ray's UFO Avoidance Rule #1, "Go in the opposite directions of strange lights spotted while driving on dark, isolated roads, especially forest roads", Travis and company inexplicably *followed* the strange yellow-orange lights. Travis says his "eye was caught by a light coming through the trees on the right, a hundred yards ahead." Because of the direction he was looking he initially assumed that the glow was the sun going down in the west. Then he thought it might be "the light of some hunters camped there — headlights or maybe a fire." Another excited truck occupant thought it was a "crashed plane hanging in a tree". As they got closer they were "electrified by the most awesome, incredible sight" they had ever seen. Indeed it was. Fellow truck mate Allen Dalis, exercising the finely tuned observational skills of a newbie woodsman yelled "It's a flying saucer!"

Then blatantly ignoring Ray's UFO Avoidance Rule #2, "Once the UFO is spotted, make haste in the other direction - screaming like a little girl is optional"- Mike Rogers brought the truck to a sudden skidding halt a few dozen yards away from the saucer. As time stood still, the truck's captive occupants all observed a golden-glowing, classic disc-shaped UFO, 15 to 20 feet in diameter, hovering solidly only 15 feet above a pile of "logging slash." The craft made no noise and the forest went silent. It lit up the immediate area of the forest with an eerie yellow light while the truck's occupants began to instinctively react, some making vastly better decisions than others.

Ken Peterson screamed "Damnation, this is really happening!" Tough guy, Allen Dalis, displaying maturity far beyond his years and a superior appreciation for the grave situation at hand, tried hiding by ducking down between his knees. The rest of the crew was simply dumbstruck except for proven daredevil Travis Walton who was about to make history.

Wantonly ignoring the most important UFO avoidance rule ever crafted, Ray's UFO Avoidance Rule #3, "NEVER willingly approach a glowing, hovering UFO", Travis Walton left the truck and slowly approached the glowing craft which hung motionless ahead. His truck mates started to lose their last ounce of sanity while they watched Travis gaining on the "smooth unblemished surface of the curving hull".

Although the truck was full of screams telling Travis to leave the object alone and get back inside they failed to alter his momentum. Even that quintessential buddy-bonding accolade "That crazy son of a bitch!" failed to take Travis off his mission which was clearly to get an up close and personal view of the bottom of the craft; crazy son of a bitch indeed!

When he was within just a few feet of the craft, crouching down low, Travis could hear a mix of high and low pitch mechanical sounds. There was also a strange mix of high-pitched beeping sounds and the low rumbling of heavy machinery. Now at his closest point to the craft, nearly directly underneath it, he heard a distinct increase in vibrational sounds and noticed the craft was beginning to wobble. At that moment his cosmic curiosity was now fully satisfied and Travis was standing up to make a turn and get the devil out of there. As a famous bungling secret agent used to say "he was *that* close!"

While he was slowly rising from his crouched position Travis was hit by a blinding, blue-green ray that emanated from the bottom of the craft. His stunned fellow loggers watched in horror as the foot-wide beam hit him in the upper body with a sharp cracking sound, delivering a high-voltage, electrocution-like blow. Travis's body arched backwards, was lifted off the ground, and thrown backwards several feet. Upon landing his motionless body caused his co-workers to go into a panic, some demanding that the driver "Get this son of a bitch moving." Driver Mike Rogers didn't need any motivation from his newly terrorized employees, he'd also seen what happened to Travis and he floored the truck away from both the weaponized craft and the apparently mortally wounded Travis Walton.

The NatGeo stump is a silent witness to the Travis Walton experience.

This is the Ground Zero ridgetop for the Travis Walton experience south of Heber, AZ. The truck he was riding in along with 6 co-workers was on a nearby forest road which is no longer in use today. As they were heading southwest on that road Travis had a clear western view up to this small ridge that was hosting unexpected intergalactic visitors in a glowing craft; they would soon take Travis for a once-in-a-lifetime adventure. Researchers and documentary makers had marked specific trees within the abduction site as seen on the stump in front middle.

Negotiating a Visit to the Travis Walton Site

The International UFO Congress, held frequently in Arizona, always features a Who's Who List of UFO researchers as their speakers. UFO royalty not selected as speakers will often have a table in the Expo for the purpose of selling and autographing books and for general schmoozing with the their adoring fans.

My experience has been that the entire UFO community spectrum is very generous with their time and knowledge. The UFO problem is deep and wide with sightings, implants and abductions and there is always room for more researchers who are willing to apply their intellect to a solution. UFO researchers cooperating with other UFO researchers is the norm rather than the exception and is the likely reason I wound up with Travis Walton in my 4x4, slipping and sliding on the muddy wet winter roads thru the Apache-Sitgreaves National Forest.

While discussing my post-conference plans to visit Heber with a wonderfully spiritual presence named Grace, she suggested I join her group for dinner where there would be some people who might be able to help me.

By the time I arrived at the table there was one seat remaining and it was dead center, compliments of Grace who knew I would be late and graciously saved it for me. Either that or no one wanted to sit next to my friend, Paul Davids. (Sorry Paul!) Either way, I found myself seated across from Grace and next to Paul, the executive producer and co-writer of the Showtime movie *Roswell* and a superb close up magician. Further to my right was Jennifer Stein whose movie *Travis: The True Story of Travis Walton* would win the *Best UFO Feature Film* and the *People's Choice Award* that week at the Congress's movie festival. And lo and behold, who should be seated one more chair over, Travis Walton himself, star of Jennifer's new movie.

At that very moment my brain went into overdrive. With my planned search for the Walton site eminent, there was *the* guy who could tell me exactly where it was *if* I could convince him to share his most prized possession. Fate, I need you now!

Left, front to back: Travis Walton, Jennifer Stein, Paul Davids, Author, James Rigney, Ruben Uriarte. Right, front to back: Kellie Weary, Donna Smith, Amy Gordon, Grace Schuler.

As a result of this fortuitous dinner outing, Jennifer Stein introduced me to Travis and negotiated a tentative agreement to have him accompany me to his experience site the week after the UFO Congress. We would do a post-production research project and photo shoot for potential editing into Jennifer's movie *Travis*. I could only shake my head with disbelief at my wonderful luck of being in the right place at the right time, thanks to Grace, and actually having listened for once to that voice in my head that told me to bring my pro photo equipment while packing my bags.

With that miracle completed I could sit back and watch Paul Davids perform a series of entertaining magic tricks much to the delight of all. I had known Paul prior to this evening as he and I had collaborated on some sleight of hand magic we unsuccessfully tried on the Air Force a few years prior. That humorous and enlightening story appears in the *Wright-Patterson* chapter later in this book. Spoiler alert, we almost got away with what cosmic history would have recorded as the greatest UFO researcher-triumphs-over-government coup *ever*.

Jennifer Stein won *Best UFO Feature Film* and the *People's Choice Award* for her documentary *Travis*. No surprise, Travis was the star.

Several times throughout the remaining days of the Congress, I ran into Jennifer and Travis, both studiously working together to promote their movie. At each meeting Jennifer raised the issue of Travis and I returning to his experience site and doing the research and the photo shoot. Travis deftly deferred at each of these casual encounters, citing other professional commitments. Caught in the middle I tried to remain both understanding and diplomatic, exchanging phone numbers with Travis and agreeing to check in with him from time to time before I left for Heber. I was going there with or without him but hoped in desperate silence that he could clear his schedule. I booked a four wheel drive vehicle to deal with the wet and hilly forest roads and planned for the worst, no Travis.

It was my good fortune to run into Jennifer one last time as I waited for the shuttle to take me from the hotel to the rental car agency at the airport. The conference was over and she was going to meet with Travis one more time before heading home. When I contacted Travis later that day from my hotel in Heber he had apparently fallen victim to Jennifer's endless charm and persistent cajoling and agreed to meet with me in Heber the following day for our pre-discussed field trip. I was definitely excited about doing a research project with Travis at the location of his famous incident, but that little nagging voice in the back of my head was giving me cautionary messages. Would he actually show up to work with this UFO tourist and reveal his secret site yet again?

At 10 am on the morning of our planned excursion, the weather in Heber, Arizona, was all sunshine and balloons after early morning light snow flurries left a white angelic dusting on the surrounding pine forest. When I called Travis at our pre-arranged time he had apparently overslept, was no longer under Jennifer's invigorating influence, and tried to cancel the outing due to "inclement weather conditions in Heber."

Looking out my hotel room window, situated in Heber, I assured him that the weather there was absolutely perfect for our plans and threatened to send him *and* Jennifer a photo of the deep blue sky; hell hath no fury like a movie producer scorned!

Stressing the importance of our upcoming work to his movie's editorial process, I offered to stay an extra day if that's what it took for the weather to sufficiently improve to tough woodsman standards. Apparently sensing my sincerity, and possibly realizing that I'd rat him out to Jennifer in a New York minute, Travis eventually caved and agreed to arrive in three hours; he was still in the Phoenix area. Drat.

I should have known that rock stars sleep in late. Sigh. I also should have known that the weather at high elevation is fickle in February and is apt to change. No sooner did I hang up the phone with Travis, after expounding on the glorious local weather conditions, then the sky began to cloud up and snow began to spritz. Oh well, not my problem. I had three more hours to prepare for a once-in-a-lifetime photo shoot and Travis was on his way. I was just hoping he didn't have a good weather app on his smartphone to call my bluff.

As pristine as the driven snow, my rental car is parked at the hotel in Heber, AZ, awaiting the arrival of Travis Walton and a guided visit to his Apache-Sitgreaves National Forest UFO encounter site. A later photo bears witness to the treacherous road that is the route to Walton's Ufologically significant location.

Travis Goes Missing: His Crewmates Contact Authorities

Having seen Travis hit by an energy beam of some sort and watching his body fly thru the air, the truck's occupants all feared for their lives as they sped away from the scene. It took them several minutes to regain their composure and locate their "man cards", whereupon someone suggested they return for Travis and get him some much needed medical attention.

While the truck was stopped a heated debate ensued about where the truck should go next, back to get Travis or into town to get the Sheriff. Mike Rogers broke the stalemate by emphatically stating he was going back to find Travis and the weak-hearted could wait in the dark with the mountain lions and black bears for his return; no one accepted his dictatorially democratic offer. Unfortunately, by the time the crew returned to the site where they had last seen Travis and the glowing craft, both had vanished.

Mike Rogers and his crew immediately conducted a quick yet extensive search by illuminating the area with the truck's headlights and searching the fringes with a solitary flashlight. One critical problem they were facing is no one was certain of the exact spot where Travis had received his high-voltage jolt. They could not find any physical evidence left behind by the craft or any footprints which might help to narrow the search area.

After carefully searching what they thought was the target area they made a group decision to head for Heber and contact the authorities to report a missing person. Exactly *what* they were going to say was debated profusely in the truck until the moment they stopped at a public phone to make the call. Even then they held back one small critical part of the story, the appearance of that pesky little UFO thing. Ken Peterson simply told the Sheriff on the phone that one of their crew was missing. What a surprise lay in store for Deputy Ellison when he arrived 45 minutes later to take the crew's entire story!

When Deputy Ellison arrived he found six men whose faces bore the total tale of their terror. In turn and often in unison, they let out an excited volley of words describing the remarkable event they had all just witnessed. After Ellison listened carefully to the fantastic story unfolding in front of him, he decided the best course of action was to call in reinforcements to start looking for the missing Travis; he'd deal with the UFO stuff later.

At this intersection in Heber, Arizona, the logging crew found some public phones and called Deputy Ellison to report a missing Travis Walton. An expanded view from this location, shown later, reveals a heretofore undocumented connection between the telephone used by the crew and the telephone used by Travis upon his return.

Within the hour, Ellison had Sheriff Marlin Gillespie and Undersheriff Ken Coplan on site to question the crew and join the search party. Taking Ken, Mike and Allen with them, the law officers returned to the "scene of the crime" to do an extended and ultimately futile search for Travis. Things were not looking good for the missing woodsman nor his traumatized crewmates; the clock was ticking.

According to Travis Walton, who was in my car at the time of the declaration and pointing to the phones in the next photo, they are the ones that were used by crew member Ken Peterson to call Deputy Sheriff Ellison when the crew reached Heber after Travis's untimely disappearance. There is no doubt in my mind that Travis was pointing to the phones used by his crewmates on the night of his disappearance. But that brings up another issue.

In Chapter 4, first paragraph of Travis's *Fire in the Sky* he states that "Ken Peterson's breath fogged up the cold glass" of the phone booth while Mike and Allen were "just outside the booth." Obviously these are *not* "phone booths." When I questioned Travis on this point he admitted he mistakenly assumed the crew used the same phones he did when he was returned and wrote the story accordingly. Although he learned of the phone booth mistake after the fact, the error was never corrected in his book and no one *ever* pointed out the book's failure to match reality, *until now*. Hopefully, this will not be my greatest contribution to the hallowed annals of UFO history.

It is easy to drive right by these phones without seeing them since they are often obscured by the service trucks assigned to the building.

Travis Appears, So Do the Wild Horses

It was 2 pm when, without warning, Travis Walton magically reappeared in Heber, Arizona, in the parking lot of my hotel. We would have about four hours of daylight to get to his abduction site, find our targets, take the photos and get down the mountain by sunset. After reading the book on his abduction and researching other sources for over a year, wild horses could not keep me away from my date with UFO history. Then again, don't ever underestimate the power of wild horses.

Although I had memorized all directional materials to Travis' site and some written copies of same were close at hand, Travis readily volunteered to act as a human GPS and call out the few turns necessary to get us to our special destination. Quickly leaving pavement out of Heber we found ourselves on slick roads covered in about 3 inches of mud, all compliments of that day's intermittent snow flurries which I had told Travis "did not exist." OK, I'll admit it, all Air Force people are taught to say that.

Meanwhile, the 4 x 4 easily negotiated the flat surfaces at slow speed; the steep hills were another story, much like an out of control travelling carnival ride. I had never driven off-road-style on-road but quickly realized it was exactly like negotiating the ice and snow-covered streets of my hometown in Detroit, except for all those pine trees lining the road. We didn't get many of those lining the oily streets of the Motor City, only dying Elm trees, the disastrous victims of a nationwide plague, Dutch elm disease.

Once I got the hang of driving on slippery dense mud, my SUV never went more than 45 degrees sideways, and the color simultaneously returned to Travis's well-tanned face and his phenomenal mustache. As he tried his best to relax in his seat, his hand still clinging to the overhead handle, Travis began to relate life in the forest as a woodsman and as a member of Mike Roger's logging crew. He pointed out the boundaries of the tree thinning contract they were working back in 1975 when he was abducted and told stories of the crew chasing large elk with their truck on their way to work. Strange behavior? Not Really. What outdoorsman amongst us wouldn't enjoy a little morning elk hunt in a pickup truck in the middle of the secluded forest?

Yeah, I know, chasing monstrous elk in a ten-year-old truck filled with wild-eyed woodsman, explosive gasoline cans and heavy chain saws over gigantic bumps in the road sounds a bit sketchy. But then I thought, when compared to the actual abduction story it sounds absolutely mainstream Heber, Arizona, and I kept driving. Until of course I was stopped by, you guessed it, the proverbial wild horses.

****

I'm not making this up. They have an Elk Crossing in the Apache-Sitgreaves National Forest.

****

Under the highly unusual circumstances of slippery road, UFO rock star in the front seat and being in a former UFO visitation and abduction area, my senses were not on high alert, they were on hyper drive. It's no surprise then that the sudden kaleidoscopic movement that caught my peripheral vision left me almost breathless and the SUV nearly heading off the treacherous road. I brought the vehicle to a sliding stop, caught my breath and pointed to the rocky hillside about 150 yards to the north.

From the vehicle I could see several majestic wild horses grazing on the remaining winter grass at the base of the hill. There were white ones, black ones, dark brown ones, light brown ones and combinations of these colors. Thankful that the 4x4 had stayed on the road and my well-travelled passenger was not complaining about my driving skills, I instinctively said the first thing that came to my increasingly overstimulated brain.

"Do you want to get out?" Yes, I had momentarily forgotten Travis's recorded UFO history when I hazardously asked this question.

He answered "Do you?"

Without hesitation I replied "You betcha!"

Immediately I had the strongest and strangest case of déjà vu I had ever experienced.

Almost too casually Travis said "Did you know that wild horses can stomp you to death?" No, that's not the déjà vu I was talking about. Wait for it...

Without a nanosecond of hesitation, and not waiting for my reply, Travis was headed out of the SUV and heading straight toward the athletic looking herd. My brain suddenly ceased to function normally while I tried to get my head around exactly what was happening right in front of me.

History shows that Travis's personal record, when impulsively abandoning the safety of a truck in the Apache-Sitgreaves National Forest in the presence of obvious and imminent danger is, well, less than stellar. And the consequences of those impulsive actions are well documented; five days of indescribable physical contact with extraterrestrials. *That's* the déjà vu I'm talking about.

Knowing his history by heart my first instinct was to yell, just like his crewmates, "Travis, you crazy son of a bitch, get back here!"

Let the record show that, while it was one of the toughest temptations I've ever encountered, I resisted the urge to be historically and monumentally cliché.

Instead I hastily departed the mud splattered vehicle to join him as he crossed the *Valley of Death* residing between us and the snorting herd. All the while a string of adrenalin-induced outrageous questions made their way through my now expanding cranium while I reluctantly conceded that I was part of whatever happened next. What follows is a brief accounting of this temporary insanity, possibly induced by the fresh mountain air.

As Travis closed the distance between us and the herd I asked myself, "How close is he actually going to get to those potentially human-stomping horses?" Considering what he did with the spacecraft in November 1975, I was fully expecting him to try to hitch a ride on one of these noble steeds. Considering my driving exhibition that day he may have considered it a safer choice.

Then I thought, "If the horses *do* try to trample him, do I run back to the car or do I take photos of the event and retire early?" Spoiler, take the pictures *then* run; I'm already retired!

Travis had told me that as a younger man he was a good sprinter. So I thought, "If the horses charge both of us, can I outrun *the* Travis Walton?" After all the horses may only need to stomp one person – survival of the fittest and all that. So I'm thinking, I'm a veteran multi-marathoner, ran Boston twice, but those alien friends of his may have endowed him with some unrevealed super powers like The Flash and I didn't want to be caught by surprise as he blasted past me and left me to have a Tim Burton-esque horse carousel nightmare.

Then I thought, "If we make it back to the vehicle alive *and* the vehicle is trampled by the wild horses, how would I explain the exterior hoof prints and interior poop smell to the rental car agency?" "You see, sir, I was with this guy from Snowflake who once spent five days on an alien space ship. Yeah, that's right, that crazy son of a bitch, Travis. Anyway, we were just sneaking up on these wild horses and the funniest thing happened..."

That entire internal discussion was started and finished by the time I snapped the telephoto lens onto the camera body, slid out of the driver's seat and made my way toward the herd. I caught up to the quickly moving Travis and for several minutes we took pictures and watched the herd quietly graze. On this occasion they did not seem to notice us at all, probably because we, just me actually, made sure to keep our distance. It was quite a different story after we finished our photo shoot assignment and engaged the herd a second time later that day.

Only Wild Horses could delay our mission. Or one Travis Walton shooting the herd with his ever present camera before making a hasty retreat to the safety of the 4x4.

Sometimes "X" Does Mark the Spot

From this point forward the road was more forgiving and I was advised to go very slowly as to not slide past the turn off to our destination. I was silently celebrating when Travis told me to turn at a location that was marked by a small strand of yellow police tape normally found at the scene of the crime – how appropriate. The turn off was precisely where I had researched it to be, a designated distance beyond a landmark I discovered and I hoped would still be in place when I arrived nearby; it was!

The old forest road we entered looked exactly like hundreds of other unused, overgrown logging roads throughout the Apache-Sitgreaves National Forest. Further disguising this special path was the snow which had fallen throughout the day and the increased tree population over the last 40 years since the path was last used commercially. I actually stopped twice along the way thinking that we'd reached the end of the navigable terrain. Each time I hesitated Travis pointed a knowledgeable finger in the right direction and I continued squeezing the vehicle through clusters of pines, advancing several more yards towards the top of the ridge. When we finally came to a complete roadblock of trees, which to me was the end of the road, I looked over at Travis who gave me one of those devil may care "hey, it's *your* rental car" looks. It was time to park it.

True to form, I had barely turned off the ignition when Travis flung open the door, exited the vehicle and headed straight up the small hill in front of us. By the time I grabbed my camera equipment, snapped one picture, put my coat on and retrieved the ladder from the rear compartment, Travis had disappeared. Again!

A Day with Travis Walton

I know what this may look like but it's actually Travis Walton about to disappear into the Sitgreaves National Forest. And not for the first time I might add. This is the gateway to the site of his abduction experience of 5 November 1975.

Searching for Travis Walton

The official search party gathered at the Exxon Station in Heber and awaited Travis's crew from the day before and two of his brothers, all driving in from Snowflake. The group of fifty men included the Sherriff's posse, the Navajo County Search and Rescue Team and U.S. Forest Service employees, most of whom were outfitted with four-wheel-drives or large government trucks. When they reached the search zone they lightly spread out and covered nearly every inch of terrain, looking for any clue the missing man may have left behind. Instead, they found a useless mountain of debris of discarded cigarette packs, oil cans, pop bottles and pieces of exhaust pipe. Unless Travis had suddenly become Goober of Mayberry this debris had nothing to do with his disappearance.

The desperate search effort continuously widened in scope and intensity over a four day period as helicopters, spotters in fixed-wing aircraft and men on horseback were belatedly added to the team. These extra and expensive resources combed dozens of additional square miles around the original abduction site including land south of the Rim Road on the Apache Reservation; ostensively because injured animals typically travel downhill. I will never understand Native American logic.

Despite having all the resources necessary to survey a relatively small geographical area, not one relevant clue was discovered about the missing person. On Sunday evening the horses and flying machines were sent away and the search was unceremoniously terminated by an exhausted and resigned Sheriff Gillespie. Everyone who had worked so tirelessly on the search teams wondered aloud "Where was Travis Walton?"

Where was Travis Walton?

That's exactly what I was thinking as I slammed the SUV's door, looped the step ladder over my shoulder, and hit the electronic door lock button; can't be too careful out there with aliens and their like running around. Unlike the original search and rescue effort in 1975 I knew what direction Travis was heading and could find an occasional footprint in the light snow. I followed the trail for a hundred feet or so, broke through a strand of young snow-covered pine trees and spotted my prey studying a tree trunk that had apparently been cut down long ago.

"This is one of the tree stumps. Make sure you get a picture of it" Travis said, resolutely.

So noted and I obliged.

For over an hour we repeated this scenario where Travis found a severed tree trunk of interest and I took photos of its rings accompanied by my museum piece compass. Our objective was to gather evidence that the craft which abducted Travis had a measureable impact on the growth rate of the nearby pine trees in the form of accelerated growth in the direction of the craft. This evidence, if revelatory, would then be considered for inclusion in the next edit of Jennifer Stein's award winning movie, *Travis*. The seemingly simple task of identifying and photographing tree stumps was not without its potential show stopping problems, all compliments of Mother Nature.

The first problem we encountered was located on top of every target tree stump, a thick mixture of ice and hardened snow which had to be carefully removed prior to photographing. I emphasize "careful" here because the second problem was the physical condition of many of the stumps which was dreadful.

Dead wood left out in the elements deteriorates quickly and so was the case with the majority of our forest "models" that day. In my opinion we found only three stumps that were old enough and retained enough physical integrity to provide definitive evidence for this mini research effort; hardly enough data upon which to make a scientific conclusion. I would have given my kingdom for a tree saw of any design to cut some additional trees for evaluation; maybe next time.

Searching for evidence that the trees near the hovering craft grew at an accelerated rate "in the direction" of the craft. Several trees did exhibit an apparent unusual accelerated growth in the predicted direction. Two of those trees are pictured next.

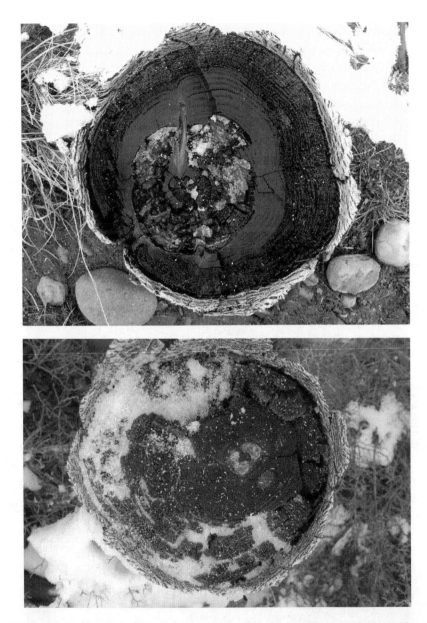

Unusual, accelerated, directional growth towards the landing site is evident on these tree stumps and several more in the immediate area.

A Personal Tour of UFO History

Imagine joining your favorite celebrity for a personally guided tour of the site that defines them today, Michelangelo in the Sistine Chapel, Thomas Edison at his Menlo Park laboratory, or Tom Cruise in Kelly McGillis's *Top Gun* boudoir. I know, two of these guys are no longer with us, and Kelly McGillis is now a lesbian, but I did say *imagine*. Such was the case when Travis Walton gave me the gold tour of the site from which he was mysteriously extracted by forces that only he can explain. Standing in the middle of the site, high on the ridge, my host pointed and waved his arm eastward to the shallow cut immediately below.

Travis spoke calmly. "We were driving along a dirt road down there which no longer exists. I noticed an unusual light coming through the trees right about where we are standing now and I pointed it out to everyone else. None of us were really sure what we looking at but it was different enough to cause us to get closer."

I had read his book. I saw his movie. I knew his story. But I was riveted!

"When the truck stopped I got out and made my way right up through there", tracing an imaginary path up the hill with his finger.

"I got up close to the craft, right around there, and the next thing that happened I was struck by a ray that blew me backwards and unconscious." Travis's voice trailed off into the silence that was the Apache-Sitgreaves National Forest in late winter on a cold, overcast afternoon.

We both stood there for several moments, silently reliving the historical events that had taken place nearly forty years ago. I was clearly at the top of the UFO Mountain and loving every second.

*   *   *   *   *

The author and Travis bonding in the Apache-Sitgreaves National Forest several miles south of Heber, Arizona, at the site of Travis Walton's well known 1975 disappearance from planet Earth.

National Geographic has sponsored a couple of Travis Walton site investigations. During one of these visits they cut down some trees and took core samples of a few more to observe the growth rings and other visible anomalies contained therein.

This core sample tree is next to the Travis/Author photo site above.

Travis Returns

Five days and six hours after he disappeared from the ridge pictured above, located in the Apache-Sitgreaves Forest, Travis Walton was "returned" to the middle of the highway just west of Heber, Arizona. As he lay on the cold pavement he could see the craft that returned him hovering just a few feet off the ground. Comparing the object to the width of the road he estimated it to be about forty feet in diameter and fourteen feet in height. When it departed it did so by silently shooting vertically into the sky and disappearing from sight in an instant. From his lonely position on this freezing November evening Travis would have to complete the remainder of his historic trip home mostly by himself.

Slowly lifting his groggy head off the pavement and gaining his wobbly feet, Travis ran eastward on the highway towards Heber where he thought he saw lights in the distance. He failed to get entrance to the first set of buildings he encountered so he continued further to the Exxon station closer to town where he found a working phone booth. He called his sister's home and convinced his brother in law, Grant, who answered the phone, that he was *the* Travis Walton and not some crank caller. Within the hour Travis was joined at the phone booth by Grant and his brother Duane who made him aware for the first time exactly how long he was missing, five days. Travis thought he had only been gone for one.

*   *   *   *   *

The snow was beginning to spritz heavier. The oddly refreshing winter wind was picking up in velocity and very little daylight remained in front of the drive back to Heber. In the continuing silence I imagined the moment Travis was taken aboard the unknown craft and had his injuries assessed by its strange occupants. As we stood there in the fading daylight his troubled facial expression told me that Travis was mentally reliving those terrifying memories and I was somehow channeling his innermost thoughts.

I would have stood there until the sun came up, contemplating this mystery of the universe and acknowledging the moment in the deep quiet of the woods, reliving history. But Travis had other ideas.

"I do regret that it happened" he said, almost apologetically for breaking the silence.

I stopped taking pictures.

"If I could do it all over again I would stay in the truck." Then more silence.

This was a perfect opening for a perfect segue, a gift from Travis. We had been out in the rapidly degrading elements for a considerable length of time, it was snowing more and getting colder, Travis was in business attire except for a leather coat, and I needed just a few more photo backups before wrapping it up.

With an ironic smile on my frosty face I held out the car keys to Travis and said "This is your chance to stay in the truck. Why don't you start it up and turn on the heat. I'll be along shortly."

Of course, the comedian in me wanted to finish this brief conversation with "and try not to get abducted this time, OK?"

However, I had already surrendered my keys and it was a long, muddy run back to civilization in the increasing cold and the fading daylight. I was also unsure what month the local black bears arise from hibernation in Heber, Arizona. Despite the fact that the appearance of a black bear would definitely motivate me to a new running personal record, I just didn't see any glory in becoming the second man to disappear from within the Apache-Sitgreaves National Forest, especially since it was almost dinner hour.

The former Exxon service station in Heber where Travis Walton found a phone booth he used to call family members, who then retrieved him five days after his disappearance. The phone booths were originally on the left side of the building but were moved next to a local business for preservation purposes.

Present day defacement reads "1-800-ET Phone Home" on Travis Walton's phone originally at Heber Service station above.

Travis's First Hours after The Return

Still dazed by his close encounter and nursing his injuries, Travis was initially astounded when his brother Duane revealed that he had been gone five days. That feeling quickly changed to acceptance when Travis weighed himself in his mom's home where Duane had hid him away; he had lost ten pounds and was ravenously hungry and thirsty. Working with remarkable speed Duane arranged for Travis to be assessed by two physicians in Phoenix the next morning and then to be debriefed by Sheriff Gillespie in the evening, all without tipping off the media.

In short order Duane arranged for financial support from the National Enquirer newspaper to pay for lie detector tests, medical exams, and a hypnotic regression. The lie detector test was inconclusive because Travis was in too high of a stress state for a stress test to be performed, which is what a lie detector test actually is anyway. The hypnotic regression on the other hand revealed the entire depth and breathe of Travis's on-board experience with his extraterrestrial hosts; not many of them pleasant at all.

He recalled that his return to consciousness was greeted with the excruciating pain of someone who was burned inside and out and who felt as if "he had been literally crushed." When Travis finally managed to open his eyes he looked straight up from the table upon which he was lying to discover the faces of horrible creatures looking back. Realizing that he must be aboard the craft that zapped him, he panicked and pushed one of the three creatures present into another, perhaps inventing what is now known as *alien bowling*.

After making a mess of the ship by throwing medical equipment and utensils all about, and temporarily escaping the creatures, Travis briefly roamed the craft in search of an escape route. He was soon recaptured onboard by more humanlike beings who returned him to an operating room environment. A mask was placed over his face and he went unconscious again until he felt the cold highway pavement outside of Heber.

He's Back!

Travis suddenly returned from his latest virtual trip into the alien craft and grabbed the keys from my outstretched hand. I watched him head down the hill in the direction of the SUV towards the young stand of pine trees, stepping over multitudes of dead trees stacked like so many pickup sticks. I wondered, would he and my SUV be in the parking place when I finished my task?

It only took about fifteen minutes to wrap up the project with several more pictures and adding a large amount of notes and drawings to my notebook, not a minute too soon. The temperature took another big dip as the wind and snow picked up with intensity. It was time to head back down the hill to civilization and a warm dinner. Only wild horses or a re-vanished Travis Walton could keep me from a giant burrito in a cozy local restaurant.

I spent my final solitary minute at the abduction site taking the obligatory cell phone selfie and visualizing Travis walking up the hill 40 years earlier to get a closer look at the craft on which he would eventually spend five terror-filled days. For those sixty seconds the snow and wind abated and time seemed to stand still, a weird yet increasingly consistent phenomenon I've experienced when visiting UFO sites. This was, however, the first time I had visited a site with *the* principal protagonist who, I feared, was now back in the car devouring my emergency ration of strawberry Twizzlers.

Sure enough, by the time I got the ladder and the rest of the equipment back to the SUV, a hungry Travis had munched his way through at least half of my Twizzler stash! Oh well, better that than returning to an empty parking place in the middle of an ever darkening forest and finding only an empty candy bag and an apology note left on the ground; "Thanks 4 Twizzlers! - Travis"

I maneuvered the SUV out of the parking circle and down to the main road. We headed back down in the direction of Heber for one more mini adventure while I contemplated Travis's questionable dietary habits. I kept my extremities on my side of the vehicle lest they become a spontaneous mountain appetizer.

Retracing the road back to Heber, essentially downhill mud skiing with an SUV, we were both amazed to see the same herd of wild horses still hanging out exactly where we found them hours before.

Amazed because the Apache-Sitgreaves National Forest is over two million acres and there had to be lots of other places they could roam. So why confine yourself to just a few acres? Neither of us had a clue but that did not prevent us from rolling the dice this time and getting *much* closer to the herd than we did on our first encounter earlier in the day.

While I stood courageously distant with my camera and a 135mm lens I confidently urged Travis to get as close as possible to the grazing herd for a close up, otherwise known in the photo biz as "the death shot". Hey, the dude ate *most of* my Twizzlers!

Unlike our first encounter where the herd totally ignored our presence, this time we were definitely under the surveillance of a huge horse I called "Killer". Killer stopped eating with the rest of his buds shortly after we left the SUV. He watched us approach and rocked his head back and forth steadily as we got nearer. In an act of undeserved blind faith Travis turned his back on the herd so I could get a good pic of the moment. When he did, Killer took a few steps in our direction for the first time.

In everyone's life comes the crossroads that defines the remainder of their all too short existence. This was one of those moments.

I really wanted a photo of Killer resting his formidable chin on Travis's shoulder with a big *Mr. Ed* smile on his face. At the same time I didn't want to be the guy who dragged Travis's nearly lifeless body back to Heber awaiting another extraterrestrial miracle cure. It would be a great story, sure, but I didn't want to be part of it on that intriguing and ultimately fulfilling day.

Killer, the herd lookout, eyes intruders in his domain.

Killer's undivided attention to our position, his increasing head shaking and his slow movement in our direction let me know that we were no longer welcomed in his pasture.

Though our relative positions to the herd gave me a fifty yard head start on Travis back to the car, there was no guarantee under Obamacare that the horse could see straight enough to stomp the closest target first. I gave Travis the international hand signal for "we better get out of here because Killer is coming this way", and we hightailed it back to the SUV and Heber, slipping and sliding all the way down the mountain to pavement. They'll be no stomping today. Sorry, Killer.

"Who's weird *now*?" Travis Meets the Kardashians

By the time I got Travis back to Heber he was ravenously hungry, which was quite surprising considering he had finally finished off my whole bag of Twizzlers. (OK, I'll give it up.) On his recommendation we visited a casual restaurant that was not too distant from where he was returned by otherworldly visitors and close to the phones he used to announce his return in 1975. For a guy who's been on a spaceship and is a well-known public figure, his taste in food is downright earthly; a giant burrito and a soft drink.

Not wanting to appear as frugal as I actually tend to be, and letting Twizzler bygones be bygones, I laid out the extravagant sum of $13.00 total for both our dinners and we chowed down on the local Mexican cuisine. Although we might eventually fall victim to severe heartburn there was little chance now of getting stomped by wild horses in the dark, cold forest. Life was good.

This photo of my mud encrusted rental car was taken on the morning after our Walton site visit and subsequent burrito banquet.

On the way back to the hotel to drop Travis off at his car he pointed out the phone booth he used to call his family after being set free by the extraterrestrial visitors. Originally the phones sat next to the Exxon station but were subsequently moved to a location between two active businesses in Heber for preservation purposes. All things considered, this has to be the most famous phone booth in America since the Mojave phone booth was retired and mothballed in 2000. If there was ever a "Kodak Photo Spot for Ufology" this is it.

Located at 34° 25' 51.83"N, 110° 35' 33.92W" in Heber, AZ, these are the phones used by Travis Walton to call home when he was returned after five days spent aboard an extraterrestrial craft also seen by six co-workers. These booths were relocated from the now-closed Exxon station for preservation purposes.

The days, weeks, and months following Travis' return from space were filled with endless inquiries from around the world, everyone wanting to hear about his adventure. Perhaps tired of telling the same story over and over, in 1978 Travis detailed his experiences in a 181 page paperback book titled *The Walton Experience*. Nearly twenty years later, the book was revised and greatly expanded to include both a discussion of the movie *Fire in the Sky*, a Hollywood version of Travis's story, and a marvelous one hundred page response to any and all debunkers.

Although both editions are a very serious retelling of a very serious occurrence, in my dealings with Travis I did discover that he has a great sense of humor. There are two incidents among many that always make me laugh out loud when I think about them. The first happened almost exactly one year before my visit with him to his UFO site. The second occurred as we entered the Mexican Restaurant parking lot after our on-site photo shoot.

In 2012, crop circle cinematographer and multiple IUFOC Film Festival Award Winner, Patty Greer, introduced me to Travis at the IUFOC awards banquet. There, Travis graciously agreed to take a photo with me that I eventually used to create what I thought was a funny t-shirt to wear at the 2013 IUFOC. When I showed the shirt to Travis he had a surprisingly healthy laugh about it, signed it, and then asked me show it to a few select individuals at the conference.

Next time
PLEASE
TAKE HIM!

Travis autographed this photo I'd put on a t-shirt. He's probably thought this many times while posing for pictures the last forty years.

The other memorable merry moment occurred as we were pulling into the parking lot of the previously mentioned Mexican restaurant in Heber where Travis and I had the following unsolicited conversation. Why he brought up the subject I do not know. Perhaps the Kardashians served Mexican cuisine on the set of their TV show while he was in the house.

Out of nowhere, Travis says "Have you heard of the Kardashians?"

Not wanting to appear as if I had just crawled out from under a big rock, I replied, "Yes, of course." But I was thinking, "where the hell is he going with this?!"

Travis continued "Well, I was on an episode of the Kardashians not too long ago. Did you see it?"

I cautiously replied, "No, I'm sorry, I didn't. I don't know *how* I could have missed that." But I was actually thinking, "Shit, he really does think I'm a moron, doesn't he?"

Travis continued. "Everyone involved in the filming was super nice, on and off camera, except Bruce Jenner. Bruce was really rude to me during the shooting because that was part of the script. He was chosen to provide the drama in the episode to balance the genuine interest of the rest of his family. Off camera he was really nice; on camera he said lots of mean things to me, calling me "*weird* and all."

I just kept nodding somewhat knowingly because I was aware that Bruce Jenner had declared his intention to become a woman! The media was full of Bruce Jenner transformation photos that blew the minds of us who remember him only as a "man's man" winning the 1976 Olympic Decathlon for heaven's sake.

As I pulled into the parking space, turned off the car's headlamps and ignition, Travis dropped the long-awaited punchline to his story.

"You've seen those recent strange photos of him, right?"

I nodded "yes" and thought "Here it comes."

Then with laughing sarcasm, Travis says "Well, I want to send him a text and ask 'Who's *weird now*, Bruce?!!' "

Then he looked my way and broke into a self-satisfied grin that he usually reserves only for special occasions. If you know Travis you know what I mean.

It took me five minutes to stop laughing.

*   *   *   *   *

Hung inside a business near the current phone booth, this autographed *Fire in the Sky* movie poster reads "Hugo Flores – Thanks for rescuing the phone booths – our historic local landmark! Travis Walton"

The Final Furlong

Enjoying a delicious cup of well-deserved coffee after the photo shoot.

There is no doubt in my mind that the story Travis and his former co-workers tell about the abduction, return, and the effect on their lives is being told as truthfully as each and every one of them can recall. Today, Travis believes that he was accidentally injured by a departing craft and was taken on board so he could be healed by their advanced medical techniques. Long gone are the original thoughts that he was actually attacked by the craft and abducted for experimental purposes.

After spending several hours with Travis, on site and elsewhere, and talking about his incident and life in general I have only one burning question remaining that needs to be answered: Can I beat "that crazy son of a bitch" in a 100 yard dash?

Someday in the near future I'd like to put that question to the test, horses or no horses – and I think I'd win.

That's our story and I'm sticking to it.

Chapter Epilogues

The Phone Booths

As stated earlier in the chapter, there is a simple but as of yet, unreported relationship between the phones used by Travis' crew to call the sheriff to report his disappearance and the phones Travis used to call his sister's home to report his return.

This photo, taken next to the phones used by Travis's crew to call the sheriff on 5 November 1975, reveals how close they were to the phone used by Travis upon his return. The small white building in the background is the former Exxon service station where Travis found phones to "call home" on the night his ET friends deposited him on the highway. At the time of the incident in 1975 these two sets of phones were less than 200 feet apart! Did Travis's abductors know this was a phone-rich area before depositing him nearby?

Present Day Travis

I did bump into Travis several times at Contact In The Desert (CITD) 2015, just three months after our photo shoot in the Apache-Sitgreaves Forest. We briefly chatted near The Sanctuary building at Joshua Tree Retreat where he had a book table reserved for CITD presenters. We also chatted at the CITD speaker's party where he referred to my camera as "the magic Black Box." I'm taking that as a massive compliment.

During his presentation at CITD's *Contact Panel* he used the now familiar phrase "I regret that it happened." I suppose he's thought a lot about what life would have been had "it" not happened and prefers an alternative destiny to the one he now lives. The fact that Travis does not find it easy to smile may be a reflection of the regret he always expresses in his public appearances. Or it could be just a fence to keep out the curious.

I took the following two photos at CITD 2015, one after the Contact Panel and the other while I was casually shooting interesting structures on the Joshua Tree Resort Property. I consider it a near miracle to catch a gleaming smile from Travis. Sometimes you're just in the right place at the right time; like getting a picture of the mystical unicorn walking in the forest.

Decades after his experience Travis does not refer to it as an abduction. His reasoning is he was not targeted by the craft that fully energized and burned his body. He now believes that he was in the wrong place at the wrong time and the craft's occupants only took him on board for five days as a mercy mission, specifically to heal him of wounds they had accidentally inflicted.

Then they safely released him back into the wild.

Contact Panel at 2015 Contact In The Desert, Joshua Tree, CA.
L to R: Yvonne Smith, Kathleen Marden, Travis Walton, Victoria Gavoian,
Sherry Wilde, Robert Perala

Travis' book, *Fire in the Sky,* is a *must read.* It is 300 pages of gripping narrative, detailing his entire experience, finishing with a 100 page gem of an Appendix. Therein, Travis masterfully flays open debunker Phil Klass, and exposes all the nefarious actions Klass employed in a deceitful and ultimately failed attempt to weaken Walton's story. It's a masterpiece! Klass is dismissed!

The *Travis* Movie: Research and Photo Shoot

Per agreement with *Travis* movie producer Jennifer Stein, the author would photograph and document the tree rings of existing tree stumps that encircled the actual abduction site. The purpose of this exercise was to document any unusual growth patterns in the trees which might have resulted from their exposure to Travis's spacecraft. Afterwards, Jennifer would decide if the evidence was compelling enough to include the author's photographs in the final cut of *Travis*.

Using the tree stump that Travis called the NatGeo tree near the centroid of the search area, Travis identified several candidate tree stumps to document that encircled this central marker. The author photographed the rings of each stump both with and without a compass on the top of the stump to document the compass direction of accelerated growth. Each tree location was then plotted in the author's notebook relative to its position and distance from the NatGeo stump. Finally, the information was transferred to an aerial photo of the site as provided by Jennifer Stein and is presented on the next page.

The large photos of two tree stumps which were included earlier in this book each show the unusual accelerated growth pattern in a single direction. Since only three stumps were large enough and preserved enough to clearly and indisputably see these patterns they are included on the plotted aerial photo.

Although three trees is a very small sample, their unusual growth pattern is undeniable. And when plotted on the aerial photo as a group, the direction of accelerated growth in each is consistently in the direction of the abduction site's centroid area – tending towards the NatGeo tree. Clearly there is a need here for a more thorough inspection and evaluation of the phenomena hinted at in the author's photographs of the tree rings. May I suggest a good tree saw and permission from the Forest landlords?

It should be duly noted that no trees were harmed during the abduction site photo shoot.

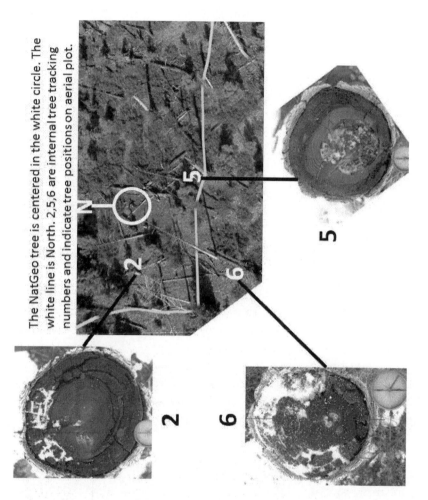

The NatGeo tree is centered in the white circle. The white line is North. 2,5,6 are internal tree tracking numbers and indicate tree positions on aerial plot.

Many tree stumps in the immediate area exhibited similar accelerated growth towards the abduction site centroid. However, their photographs are less convincing than the three largest trees presented here.

The reader will note the conspicuous absence of location coordinates for the actual Travis Walton site in this book. Travis asked me not to share the location information on the grounds that there remains today potential scientific evidence that needs to be preserved for future research. I could not agree with him more and I am a man of my word. My promise and my moral compass aside, I believe it within the spirit of our agreement to leave behind a tantalizing clue to the correct location in the photo above where the yellow tape was removed as we departed the site.

P.S. I'm over this. If not, Travis's coordinates would be listed above.

Adventure 4
Wright-Patterson Air Force Base: An Insider's Story

UFOs & Alien Mysteries
"After forty years of wandering Wright-Patterson Air Force Base looking for stone tablets, I think I finally found some." –Author

An F-15 Eagle at Wright-Patterson's Air Force Material Command Headquarters looms majestically over Air Force Marathon competitors.

Wright-Patterson Air Force Base near Dayton, Ohio, is famous for its aviation heritage and its conspiratorial connection to UFOs and Extraterrestrials. The world's first airplane pilots, the Wright Brothers, were from Dayton and did almost all of their research and development in the area. And let's not forget that Aliens were reputedly brought to Dayton along with their crashed air vehicles found in the New Mexico desert in 1947.

Countless books and articles have been written about the Wright Brothers and even more have been written about Wright-Patt's publicly revealed and sometimes secretly hidden links to UFOs and ETs. A niggling issue with previous Wright-Patt UFO/ET writings is the fact that most of the authors never worked on the base nor ever set foot there. As a result, their "new evidence" is often a rewarmed story that was obtained through "the son of the guy who spent a day on the base who told the story to his hairdresser"-tenuous information at best.

This chapter addresses that deficiency as the author is a former long-time insider, having worked on the base from January 1973 until September 2011. Herein the reader will discover new, first-person, on-base investigative experiences that qualify as original under most accepted definitions.

The intriguing and mysterious issues of alien burial sites, security force secrets, Men in Black discussing Area 51, 60 years of UFO obfuscation by the Air Force, and UFOs over Wright-Patterson are all explored as a first-person experience on Wright-Patterson. So, too, are the not so mysterious issues of beer-based UFO security breaches immediately outside Wright-Patt's UFO building, and a famous alien's attempt to return home to Wright-Patt via a cross-country road trip from Los Angeles, California.

Ladies and gentlemen, here's your backstage pass to Wright-Patterson Air Force Base insider UFO theories and evidence. It's time to rock and roll!

U2 reconnaissance plane flies over Wright-Patterson, September 2015.

Wright-Patterson Becomes Synonymous with UFOs

Wright-Patterson Air Force Base (WPAFB or Wright-Patt) is unquestionably one of the legendary sites in the world of Ufology. Its Foreign Technology Division (FTD) housed Project Blue Book, the Air Force's official yet much maligned UFO investigation project for nearly twenty years. It is widely believed to be the repository of UFO crash wreckage and alien bodies since the 1947 Roswell UFO crash.

"Wright-Patterson" has earned equal name recognition with other legendary UFO-related sites like "Roswell" and "Area 51" in large part because it has been chained to these places through documented fact and progressive, logic-based analysis.

Mere mention of Wright-Patterson will have any group of serious UFO researchers debating whether or not the well-founded rumors are true: Was the 1947 Roswell UFO crash wreckage taken to Wright-Patterson for analysis and exploitation along with both dead and living aliens? Are these recovered prized items now split between Area 51 and Wright-Patt? What was the real purpose of Project Blue Book; scientific investigation or public relations scam? Why was Senator Barry Goldwater scolded by an angry General Curtis LeMay who said "Not only can't you get into it but don't you ever mention it to me again" when Goldwater inquired about FTD's UFO holdings?

Critical to understanding Wright-Patterson's lofty stature in Ufology and the associated controversy is understanding the Roswell, New Mexico, crash and retrieval story itself along with the Air Force's long running UFO investigation, Project Blue Book, which ran from 1952 until 1969.

Had it not been for one very small mistake by an Air Force Colonel in 1947, Roswell and Wright-Patterson Air Force Base would be just another cow town in New Mexico and just another large Air Force base near Dayton, Ohio, respectively. But sometimes Fate has a sense of humor.

In brief, in early July 1947, a rancher named Mac Brazel found unusually indestructible silver-foil-like and I-beam-like material on Foster Ranch where he was working, 70 miles northwest of Roswell, NM, and took it to the Roswell sheriff's office. The sheriff turned it over to the nearby Roswell Army Air Field (RAAF) whose commander, Col. Blanchard, directed intelligence officer Major Jesse

Marcel to visit the Foster Ranch and investigate the source of the silvery material.

After Marcel returned to RAAF with a carload of the unusual material that base experts could not identify, Col. Blanchard authorized Lt. Walter Haut, the RAAF public information officer to release a news story to the local newspaper and radio station. That infinitesimally small mistake of releasing the news story changed Roswell and Wright-Patterson forever, along with anyone reading the press release in newspapers across the country.

Shortly after the story was officially released, the Roswell Daily Record newspaper headlines screamed "RAAF Captures Flying Saucer on Ranch in Roswell Region." Meanwhile, Col. Blanchard instructed Major Marcel to **"fly the materials to Wright Field" (now WPAFB)** after first making a stop in Fort Worth, Texas, then home of the 8th Army Air Force.

When Marcel arrived at the 8th Army Air Force Headquarters with the recovered materials, its commander, General Roger Ramey, was there to make sure the story went no further and told ravenous reporters that the recovered material was "a radar reflector from a weather balloon." The press bought the story, hook, line and sinker, and sold it to the public where it sat unquestioned for decades until, in 1978, researcher Stanton Friedman located Major Jesse Marcel who said "It sure wasn't part of a weather balloon."

In a 1979 interview Marcel added "We even tried making a dent in it with a sixteen pound sledge hammer. And there was still no dent in it"

It should be noted here that a sixteen pound sledge hammer would absolutely destroy any weather balloon radar reflector that was ever in the US Air Force inventory or anyone else's inventory, and especially so in 1947. Thus, Marcel's material could not have been a radar reflector.

Since Friedman's first Marcel interviews, hundreds of articles and published books containing first-person witness interviews, deathbed confessions, signed affidavits and official flight logs strongly suggest that the Roswell crash wreckage was indeed alien in nature and was sent to what is now Wright-Patterson Air Force Base; wreckage which was never publicly seen or heard from again.

The contentious debate about the nature of the Roswell wreckage and Wright-Patterson's role in handling that wreckage has raged since the publication of the first Roswell book, and still does today. Ironically, the Air Force itself is partially responsible for stirring this boiling cauldron of controversy.

The Air Force conducted a rather continuous string of three UFO investigation projects from 1947 thru 1969, known chronologically as Sign, Grudge and Project Blue Book, which were ostensibly created to investigate UFO reports and assess recovered space-originated materials. The projects were staffed in a series of offices at Wright-Patt, beginning with the Air Technical Intelligence Center and eventually arriving at the Foreign Technology Division.

Any UFO-interested person, WPAFB employees included, who could add 2 plus 2, knew all about Wright-Patt's UFO projects and Marcel's orders to fly UFO crash wreckage to the base in 1947. There is only one logical answer the UFO-savvy public could compute when they considered both of these ideas together, "Wright-Patt's Foreign Technology Division must possess the recovered alien goods!"

NASIC in 2015 is the former FTD where Roswell UFO crash wreckage was reputedly taken in 1947. With numerous entrances available to this highly secretive building it's hard to understand why Senator Barry Goldwater had so much trouble initially finding a way in.

Wright-Patterson's UFO Culture 1973: The Author Arrives

With the Roswell/Wright-Patterson history awaiting me in January of 1973, I was one of five very nervous, wide-eyed electrical engineering co-op students from the University of Detroit to arrive at WPAFB for their first professional assignment. Drawing the short straw I was assigned to the Management Operations Office in what was then Building 22 in Area B, one of three areas at WPAFB; the others were not surprisingly, Areas A & C. (For history purists there was also an Area D at the base known as Skyway Park Housing Unit which is no longer part of the base.)

My position was in a staff office supporting the Director of the Avionics Laboratory, which would become part of Air Force Research Laboratory (AFRL) in 1997 after Congress requested consolidation of Air Force laboratory resources. At that time there were several Air Force Laboratory sites located at Air Force bases across the United States, employing several thousand civilian and military personnel.

It was in the Management Operations Office that I had my first revelation regarding the possibility that aliens and their artifacts could actually be at Wright-Patterson Air Force Base, "somewhere in the tunnels." That revelatory first conversation occurred with my assigned mentor, Al, a forward-leaning GS-11 and proud owner of a loud, vintage, stress-cracked army green Corvette. Al was definitely an extrovert, unafraid to push the envelope as they say, and his inadvertent   scare-the-crap-out-of-the-new-student-employee   alien conversation with me is detailed in the opening chapter.

After Al initiated me with "we have aliens in the tunnels", I often put that conversation to the test during my initial three-month co-op assignment by asking newly trusted workplace personnel about that specific rumor. Surprisingly, the near unanimous response was always tinged with a "well everyone knows that" kind of attitude. That response was always served up with a big smile that made me think either I was entertaining that person with my naivety or they wanted to sell me the snake oil they stored in their grey-metal, civil service desk. Those were very uncertain times for me and I was never quite sure.

The important fact established here is that not one single person at that time ever said "We have no aliens here, you crazy son of a bitch." Sorry, Travis.

Not one person gave me that response. Not Doug in Accounting Services. Not Betty in Management Operations. Not the guy who ran the greasy spoon on the other side of the hangar. Zero derogatory responses. I saw lots of smiles but no denials.

Building 22, home to the author's first co-op assignment in 1973, is now Building 570. Building numbers and street names on base change. This is important to remember. The author's desk was thru the window seen above the picnic table. In 1973 Al's Corvette would have been parked right out front so he could admire it all day long.

So what does this say about the culture at Wright-Patterson Air Force Base, circa 1973? That everyone was so open-minded about aliens landing, and sometimes crashing, that they were an accepted fact? Not likely. That overly bored employees loved to titillate each other with stories of recovered aliens and their crashed craft? Again, this explanation is very unlikely.

The most plausible explanation is the base population had simply come to accept their mostly oral, tribal history that their base was *the location* for any alien artifacts, biological or otherwise, that may have been recovered by their employer. It's like New York City residents; they're not all tough but have to act that way for the tourists. Such is the fortified legend of Wright-Patterson's aliens.

What could explain such a widespread acceptance and confident attitude in the 1970's WPAFB population towards a subject that seemingly terrified the general public? I believe it was a combination of the following: a) long term exposure to the UFO topic through personal experience, local media and the WPAFB human network; b) confidence in the WPAFB UFO *system* and the personnel who were part of that system; and c) brilliant deception by the system. Let's look at the UFO-related forces that were at work in 1973 at WPAFB.

Through projects Sign, Grudge, and Blue Book, hundreds of highly qualified WPAFB personnel were officially, and sometimes unofficially, involved with the logistics, collection, analysis, and protection of UFO data and materials from 1947 until 1969. Although the Project Blue Book office was generally understaffed with a handful of people for such an important task, they could and did leverage the talent of hundreds of the world's leading technical minds and their technical equipment readily available right there at WPAFB.

Depending on the nature of the technical analysis tasks and the material being evaluated, it is logical to assume a minimum amount of physical-plant support was required. At its most subtle instantiation this support might be quietly grabbing some empty office space to serve as a project meeting room. At its most obvious level, this support might be as massive as the creation of new secure vaults or rooms requiring loud construction processes and the acquisition and placement of large, highly technical and expensive test equipment.

It takes people to do all of the hard-to-hide physical changes, people who then might be in on at least a small piece of the big UFO secret. The point is there were hundreds of WPAFB personnel involved in supporting the investigation of the UFO phenomena for decades, some directly, some indirectly and some third-person through the friend network.

Also at work here are the related issues of confidence in the *UFO system* and the system's ability to confound the truth as it did when it announced the "successful" termination of Project Blue Book in 1969. Exactly what was the WPAFB corporate UFO knowledge in 1973; four years after the Air Force closed its official UFO project and the year of my arrival on base?

It's very unlikely that the entire UFO-savvy base population had retired or transferred by the time I arrived in January 1973, just because they'd apparently won the war over those pesky UFOs as declared by Project Blue Book. Many of the personnel I talked with in my early years on base had endured a good portion of a two decade constant stream of exposure to the ET topic; it was part of their collective heritage, much like the Wright Brothers. What better way to impress a young co-op student with your personal and professional importance than to tell him about your employer's most exotic former/ongoing research project, specifically the extraterrestrials and your system's greatest intergalactic accomplishment.

I believe these people were confident in their history because they were part of a truly skillful organization; they had supreme faith that base personnel – *the system* – could get any job completed. This self-assurance was reinforced in 1969 when Project Blue Book announced they had evaluated the UFO situation and concluded that "UFOs did not pose a threat to national security." Talk about a confidence and morale booster!

Success! We did it! The system, one which we are all part of here at WPAFB, has declared we solved the problem! Let's be sure to share this exceptionally good news with any and all who arrive at the base's front gates. And this news they shared with me in 1973.

OK, so in our moment of triumph we might have ignored hundreds of documented unidentified craft defying the laws of physics, seen visually by military personnel and on radar, recorded on film, now camping out over nuclear resources, "that pose no threat to our national security"; check! But I'm part of the system and I have faith in the system!

Disregarding that for a moment I still have to ask, what about those pesky aliens, dead or alive, that we have in the tunnels?!? That question has been asked for over six decades and is still being asked today, more often than not by those who make their living seeking answers to the Extraterrestrial Question. Could these intelligent UFO/ET researchers be chasing and writing copious amounts of text about a mystery that never existed, just as the Air Force claims?

*   *   *   *   *

According to the National Museum of the US Air Force, the VZ-9AV Avrocar prototype pictured above had an operational requirement for supersonic flight (over 761 miles per hour –MPH). Since the actual top speed of the prototype in 1961, its final year of development, was measured at 35 MPH it's safe to say that the developers missed the supersonic goal by a mere 726 MPH. With these documented results in mind, it's also safe to say that neither this device nor any other in the US inventory could possibly have been responsible for hundreds of disc-shaped UFO sightings. This is highly contradictory to what many "explainers" of the UFO phenomena would have you believe.

The $64,000 Wright-Patterson Alien Question
Now $1,000,000 Due To Inflation

No less a world class UFO/ET research authority than Linda Moulton Howe once asked me the $1M Wright-Patterson Alien Question at the 2015 *Contact in the Desert* held at the Joshua Tree Retreat Center. That close encounter did not involve the usual spaceship, abduction, missing time, nor I'm happy to report, any lasting alien probe marks on my body.

A Close Encounter with famed investigator Linda Moulton Howe.

Per my modus operandi at conferences, I arrived early for the day's initial presentation to get a front row to accommodate my photography addiction. Linda Moulton Howe was the next scheduled speaker in the track and I presumed she was in a green room somewhere nearby making her final preparations.

Part way thru Grant Cameron's presentation, which I was totally locked onto because it was about rock star alien encounters, I felt a presence take the empty seat to my right. Since I was looking leftward at Grant leaning on the podium, and hanging on to every word, I failed to see that the presence who took the empty seat was none other than Ms. Howe.

Imagine my wonderful surprise when Grant took a breath and I used that opportune moment to turn to my right to see Linda's lovely smiling face. She could tell that I was genuinely stunned and delighted to see her there displaying a Cheshire cat facial expression which said to me "I bet you weren't expecting *this* now *were* you?" Indeed, not.

When Grant's session ended I introduced myself to Linda and recorded the moment in an impromptu photograph. In a rapid-fire series of questions, befitting a person of Linda's extensive experience as a world class investigative reporter, she discovered I had worked at Wright-Patterson. Without a nanosecond's delay she dropped the $1M question: "Did you see any aliens (there)?"

Of course I immediately knew that I had no conscious memory of seeing an alien at WPAFB or at the countless other military installations I had visited in my lengthy career. But since this was *the* Linda Moulton Howe standing just inches away, and I had expected her to ease into questions of this magnitude, I suddenly lapsed into a total review of my entire life's subconscious memory, much like one does just prior to an awful automobile accident. The Oz factor was clearly at work here.

If you ever have the privilege of engaging Linda in a conversation you will quickly discover that she asks *all* the questions and you give all the answers, in a heartbeat or else she moves on. Linda must have sensed that I was reliving my entire life right in front of her, in order to provide the most accurate answer possible, because she stopped asking questions and waited patiently for my answer.

Though it only took about two seconds to respond, which I now suspect is Linda's upper-limit wait time, it probably felt like a lifetime for both of us. I know it did for me. When I told her "No", she regretfully excused herself to get ready for her presentation, but not before kindly agreeing to talk later.

It's no surprise that our short follow-on conversation included more talk about Wright-Patterson and aliens. I suspect that world class researchers will still be asking the same questions a millennia from now, unless the US government loans out an actual alien to ride on a Macy's Thanksgiving Day Parade float. Or, just the right person, with just the right security tickets, with just the right evidence, goes rogue.

Maybe the next time I'm asked the $1M Question I'll say something like "I'm not sure if I've seen aliens on the base." Or, "maybe, but not directly", a distinct possibility the next section explores in the most unusual and relatively unknown WPAFB locations.

Linda Moulton Howe accepting audience adulation at CITD 2015.

Aliens and Graveyards and Chapels, Oh My!

At this point in the book, you must be aware that I support the Extraterrestrial Hypothesis as the explanation for many reported UFOs and contact experiences. No other single explanation can account for all the reported activities of this type over the last seventy years. For me, this is pretty much cased closed. We cannot be alone in the Universe. But questions remain about those decades-long stories of aliens and their artifacts at Wright-Patterson? Could they be true? And why WPAFB?

Many well-documented, Roswell alien-crash recovery stories use witness testimony to support the claim that the craft's wreckage and the aliens, dead or alive, were taken to WPAFB. Three very compelling reasons for doing so would be: 1) the type of technical expertise available there to analyze the materials; 2) the secure facilities that the base provides; and 3) a population with the highest security clearances to protect the secret.

In 1947, WPAFB was *the* leader in aerospace technology. If you had a suspected piece of a crashed alien craft in 1947, or even the whole craft itself, there was no better place on the planet to have that material analyzed. With numerous top secret projects already active on the base, there would be sufficient real estate to build or provide adequately secured facilities to perform the analysis on pieces of material that have been described as being "no larger than three feet in length."

Most of the leading-edge aerospace technology developments were ongoing or managed at Wright-Patterson by people with the highest security clearances that could easily be upgraded to include protecting the alien secret. It was an ideal location to bring suspected wreckage from an alien craft, occupants and all. An informal poll of former co-workers seems to bear that out.

Each and every former Wright-Patterson co-worker that I ever posed the question to has agreed that the base would have been *the place* to bring the crash material and aliens. What they have mildly disagreed on was the final disposition of the aliens, dead or alive. What would we do with aliens in our possession as members of the curious and fragile Earth-bound human race?

It would be logical to assume that we would study the aliens in an attempt to find out everything about them that we possibly could. We would do this because our very survival might be dependent upon our discoveries. After all, there are thousands of reports of physics-defying spacecraft that are far superior to anything we might have in the next 1000 years, whose big-eyed owners have already discovered us. As history demonstrates, the race that is "discovered" is the race that does not fare too well; just ask the Native Americans in the United States, present day casinos notwithstanding.

Live aliens would certainly provide planet Earth with the most useful information once we were able to communicate with them. Could live aliens have been brought to WPAFB? Certainly, and for the same reasons previously stated, secure facilities and available technical expertise. But how would we care for those unfortunate creatures that did not survive the crashes?

The majority opinion of personally polled WPAFB employees is, dead aliens recovered in the present day would be kept in a preservation facility for further study, but not necessarily on WPAFB; most probably Area 51.

Regarding the aliens recovered in the late 40's and early 50's, the majority opinion is, after they were first examined to the maximum extent possible and could no longer provide useful scientific information, the deceased former star travelers were given a Christian burial somewhere on or near WPAFB!

Why would anyone even consider a Christian burial as an acceptable option rather than fully destroying the potentially incriminating evidence? Because that's the way we do things on this lonely planet.

Is Christian burial even possible on Wright-Patterson? The answer is a definite "yes."

Consider the following tantalizing fact. There are multiple verified and suspected burial sites on or immediately adjacent to Wright-Patterson. All of these could easily have served as alien burial sites without a significant chance of public discovery.

The verified human burial sites include one on the north end of the active runway, one that is located immediately adjacent to a former main gate, and one next to the former Foreign Technology Division, home of Project Blue Book; hard to believe but demonstrably true. The first undeniable evidence of these sites is shown in the next photograph and is discussed at length later in the text.

Speculative burial sites include one inside of or next to the recently demolished Chapel One, whose reputed graves may have been recently and secretly moved, and one burial site near a single family home often accommodating a multiple star general.

Ladies and gentlemen, please put your tray tables and seatbacks in their fully upright and locked positions. Please fasten your seatbelts tightly across your lap. Please stow any erroneous preconceived notions you might have about Wright-Patterson Air Force Base. It's time to land on the base and take an unprecedented discovery walk.

*   *   *   *   *

This gravesite is but a few hundred feet from the FTD building (now NASIC) at WPAFB. Could aliens have been buried here?

*   *   *   *   *

During the heyday of the Air Force's Project Blue Book, the project was housed for many years in the Foreign Technology

Division (FTD) at WPAFB. Blue Book's publicly stated objective was to investigate and explain the multitude of UFO reports received from the general public and sometimes from their own military brethren.

A close review of Project Blue Book's reports and operational history indicates that its small staff was chronically overwhelmed with reported UFO sightings, too many to thoroughly investigate by themselves. Their sketchy report conclusions and questionable public announcements regarding many high profile cases clearly indicate Blue Book had long abandoned any serious investigative work for public consumption to become a public relations endeavor; mostly aimed at calming a nervous populous with often untenable explanations.

Due to the limited nature of their charter and without a "need to know", Project Blue Book staffers would not be privy to the permanent disposition of recovered alien artifacts and dead alien bodies once the scientists had completed their investigations. That responsibility would likely fall to another group within the same FTD organization, specifically set up to handle the real scientific investigations, not the public relations versions. With deceased aliens to securely dispose of, this group would have to seriously consider the extremely close proximity of their alien storage facility to the first burial ground of interest.

At approximately 34°48'00.91"N, 84°03'14.82W you can find the small graveyard, pictured next, provided you have permission to enter WPAFB or you have Google Earth. You will notice a few vehicles in a parking lot which adjoins this site. Those vehicles are parked in the FTD (now NASIC) parking lot which is only about 500 feet from the FTD building, the long argued home of recovered aliens!

The close proximity of a highly protected, convenient burial site next to *the* building where alien artifacts and bodies were reputedly accommodated is a conspiracy theorist's Holy Grail. If alien bodies were resident in the FTD building, or one of many nearby buildings, and a final high-level decision was made to provide a proper Christian burial, there is possibly no more opportune place on the planet for that burial than in the graveyard pictured next.

This is the same graveyard as shown in a prior photo. The seasonal change reveals former FTD building in the background.

If the high command decided to lay our intergalactic guests to rest, what might the ceremony have looked like? It is easy to visualize that special arrangements would be made for an alien burial at a time when the base population was largely absent, probably after working hours or on a weekend, most likely after sunset. A highly trusted and skilled backhoe operator from base Civil Engineering would surgically excavate the gravesite. The Base Chaplain would preside over a short ceremony attended by those with the proper clearances and the need to know. The grave would then be closed and all attendees would be reminded of their oath to keep the above-top-secret event a permanent secret, or else.

The participants would leave the ceremony confident that the gravesite is protected behind the security fences of a highly secure US Air Force base. Now the gravesite is under the watchful eye of nearby 24 hour, state-of-the-art surveillance equipment. Should the need ever arise to regain access to the contents of the grave, the risk of discovery, if performed at the right time, would be nil. This is largely due to the fact that the burial compartment would only have to be returned a few hundred feet, back into the confines of what has to be one of the most highly secured buildings on the base.

What if the most logical burial place, the one closest to FTD (NASIC), was eschewed for one with a more religious association? In that case, a second logical and ideal choice for an alien burial at WPAFB would be either in or around Chapel One. This smallish whiteboard building was built in 1942, so it was a standing structure with ample land available for gravesites at the time the aliens were allegedly brought to WPAFB in 1947 and beyond. It was also conveniently located for an alien burial.

Around the world it is common for religious ceremonial structures of all sizes to host burial sites, from Europe's massive Cathedrals to the smallest of chapels. Why would this religious chapel on Wright-Patterson be any different in serving its customary function? The fact is it wouldn't.

It has also been long rumored that there were gravesites at Chapel One and these rumors were forever recorded in a local newspaper article displayed later in this chapter. Unfortunately, by the time I went to investigate the Chapel One possibilities, it was gone! It had been demolished in 2014 and its *entire* grounds conspicuously bulldozed flat. The building was gone when I arrived but not so for some potential telltale and historical clues.

In person, one observes that Chapel One was situated directly across the street from Building 219, the former Regional Hospital which housed medical personnel of all stature, including doctors, nurses and medical technicians. Both of these buildings are but a minute's drive from the main runway and its receptive hangars, into which alien artifacts would have been taken prior to their journey inside of a base research building or hospital.

Chapel One was located at 39°48'51.20"N, 84°02'16.52"W.

It is relatively easy to construct a scenario where the alien bodies, both dead and living ones, are brought to WPAFB and immediately taken to an appropriately outfitted surgical room at the base Regional Hospital, most likely after business hours. Nervously waiting military medical personnel are at a heightened state of alert as they examine the newly arrived guests. Dark suited, interested parties observe the procedures closely and swear everyone to secrecy on behalf of national security. After several weeks the examinations are complete, the reports are written and the bodies readied for final disposition.

From the Regional Hospital, the containers containing the aliens that required burial could have been simply carried the mere 100 feet across the street to the burial site in or next to the Chapel. This location would have been very convenient. It would also have been the most morally appropriate site on the base since it was considered a religious and holy site. Any other deceased aliens that required long term storage rather than burial could then have been moved to dozens of other buildings which were just a minute's drive from the hospital.

With the demolition of Chapel One in 2014, and the surrounding grounds apparently fully remediated, a new mystery is created; if alien bodies *were* at that location, where are they now?

*   *   *   *   *

According to contemporary witnesses who worked in the Hospital building, it was the sight of numerous paranormal occurrences after it ceased functioning as a clinic and was converted to business offices. Disembodied voices and smoky shadow figures were the most troubling events reported by the spooked residents. They also described numerous instances where the building would be discovered with open windows in the morning after they had been fully secured the night prior.

The former Regional Hospital, on left, is across the street from the former Chapel One site which is now no more than a temporary fence and newly bulldozed ground seen on the right.

Occupants, who had departed the building after extinguishing their office lights, reported seeing those lights turned back on by the time they reached their cars in the parking lot. Most intriguing of all, "much of the activity was reported on the third floor where the operating room was." Another creepy room at the former hospital was the basement which housed the morgue at one time.

In 2008 *Stars and Stripes* interviewed a Wright-Patt Public Affairs official who told them the following story. "Five Judge Advocate Group officers had their meeting in the basement disturbed by the sounds of a loud disruptive child laughing, running and playing. All immediate attempts by the officers to locate the child or anyone who had seen a child in the building that day were met with failure; no one other than the meeting group had heard any noise resembling a child at play."

Is it possible that the spirits of the doomed interstellar tourists, who may have been surgically examined there by military medical personnel, or died there, remained at the hospital and can account for at least some of the mysterious paranormal observances made there in the ensuing years?

Large bare spot on right is former location of Chapel One. Bare patch on left is forty feet long and just over six feet wide and could have held graves prior to destruction of Chapel One and its surrounding grounds.

*　　*　　*　　*　　*

One of the better documented cemeteries on the base is the Cox Cemetery, located between Loop Road and the north end of the runway in Area C, near State Route 235. Mr. John Cox, Sr., an early settler of Greene County, established it in 1821 on the rear border of his 690 - acre farm to serve as a family plot.

The cemetery is approximately one-third acre in size and contains 80 known graves. Though no burials have reputedly been made in the plot since the late 1920s it would be one of the most secure alien resting spots on the base for multiple reasons.

To begin with, it is located at the end of an active Air Force runway. There is always some activity going on there and is under observation 24 hours a day. The runway area is surrounded by intrusion detection fencing, an additional fence to the one which surrounds the entire base perimeter. The cemetery is open only one day a year on Memorial Day when the Base Commander leads a wreath laying ceremony. Any human presence in that area on the other 364 days of the year would be as obvious as an alien attached to your face, and would be dealt with swiftly by security forces and their automatic weapons.

The Cox cemetery, located at the end of the runway, is the most secure potential alien burial location on the base. It is located behind the white fence seen in the background through the inner security fence.

The other possible WPAFB alien burial sites demanding attention are the old Fairfield Cemetery and an undocumented location near the historical Foulois House which is conveniently located only a few hundred feet west of the former Chapel One.

Before Fairborn, Ohio was Fairborn, it was two small towns called Fairfield and Osborn whose names and borders were democratically merged in 1950. Every time the local high school football team loses a game the local wags will posit that their town should have been named Osfield. Bad jokes notwithstanding, Fairfield Cemetery is located at 39° 49'12.17"N, 84°01'47.27"W, a site which immediately adjoins Gate 1 of WPAFB. It is only several hundred feet east of the former Chapel One and the former Regional Hospital.

The same scenario considered for a Chapel One alien burial ground applies here. The extremely close proximity of the Fairfield Cemetery to the ingress and examination locations of the alien bodies would make it an excellent location for their eventual interment. Its biggest drawback would be its lack of direct Air Force security which argues mildly against its use. However, since the graveyard and the base share a common fence, and the graveyard is adjacent to a main gate, it could be observed by base employees, the gate guards, and security forces on a regular basis every day.

It is possible that those who were tasked with burying the aliens used the oldest guise in the spy playbook, "the double bluff" and hid the aliens in plain sight in Fairfield Cemetery. No one would ever think of burying a prize like that in a public cemetery they'd reason, so no one would bother to look there, except me perhaps.

Fairfield Cemetery shares a lenghty fence with WPAFB's Gate 1.

A thorough search of the Fairfield Cemetery records by the author, and a thorough walkthrough, did not reveal anyone interred there with the name of ALF, Mork, Conehead, Barf, Uncle Martin or the very sneaky Al Ian Grey. This is not to say that dark suited, fedora-wearing government employees do not have a sense of humor. I'm just saying I did not find any evidence of it in the residents list of Fairfield Cemetery.

*   *   *   *   *

The final whispered alien burial site is near the Foulois House which has accommodated many of WPAFB's Base Commanders and other ranking officers. Not surprisingly, the Foulois House property is only several hundred feet southwest of the former Chapel One and the Regional Hospital. It, too, would provide an extremely convenient and safe location to inter unfortunate intergalactic visitors whose transportation system may not have been as reliable as they were led to believe by the salesman at *Jerry's Cherry Used Spaceships.*

A cursory walk around the fenced perimeter of the property by the author did not reveal any obvious gravesites like those already discussed. However it is worth mentioning that less than two hundred feet southwest from the Foulois House fence line is an unusual grave-size mound, reminiscent of the Old West, with a gravesite-size flat stone immediately at the foot of this mound. Both of these obvious landmarks sit comfortably under two nearby shade trees, looking every bit like a restful gravesite.

It is important to note that the immediate Foulois property is completely surrounded by a period-piece wrought iron fence, very reminiscent to that surrounding the burial place located in the shadow of the FTD building. An intensive walking survey of the acreage surrounding the Foulois House reveals that the "stone and mound" combination shown in the photo is unique to the area. In fact, the author could find no other exposed large stones of this type anywhere in the relatively flat, surrounding acreage, nor any additional, nearby flat-stone and mound combinations.

That said, is it just a coincidence that an obvious gravesite-looking mound on WPAFB is in a location already reputed to have burial sites and is marked by the only exposed flat stone in the entire surrounding property? It is conceivable that this is nothing more than a long forgotten property line marker, but where there is smoke there is usually fire, and this location certainly deserves more investigation

This mound and stone marker is located on Skeel Avenue, across the road from the Tennis Club.

. ＊ ＊ ＊ ＊ ＊

The Frick family burying ground mentioned in the adjacent newspaper article is *not known* to the Base Historian (AFLCMC History Office) with whom I exchanged correspondance. The Frick story in the article is similar to the Landis-Shank story recorded in a 1995 book on Wright-Patterson which states that the Landis-Shank cemetery was also relocated. The difference is the Landis-Shank was relocated in 1941 and the Frick in 1942. Also, the Frick cemetery is said to contain 8 graves while the Landis-Shank is said to have 6 graves. It is interesting to note that the Base Historian claims no knowledge of the disposal plant which is listed in the article.

From Ohio 235 you can see a cemetery within the confines of Wright-Patterson Air Force Base. It appears to be in the middle of the airfield. Why is it there?— Mrs. T. W., West Carrollton.

The fenced-in plot is the Cox f a m i l y cemetery and contains 80 descendants of John Cox, a Virginian who bought 690 acres to establish the old v i l l a g e of Osborn. Cox set aside part of an acre for family burials in 1806. G o v e r n m e n t bought the land from the Miami Conservancy in 1944 for the old Patterson Field, agreed to carefully maintain the burial plot. An older cemetery, the Frick family burying ground, contains eight graves and was uncovered by excavators in 1942. It's in back of the disposal plant at Area A. There are stories of still another cemetery near the base chapel, but if so it's unrecorded.

Could the Frick and the Landis-Shank references actually be the very same cemeteries despite the subltle differences in their written history? The Chief of Cultural Resources at Wright-Patterson posited this opinion relative to the newspaper article I forwarded to him: "I believe the cemetery they refer to as the Frick family cemetery is most likely the one we refer to as the Landis-Shank Cemetery and it is located behind NASIC's complex." Or do we have a missing set of bodies at Wright-Patt?

Yet another visual perspective at the Frick (Landis-Shank?) cemetery reveals a stone slab extremely similar to the one found at the Foulois House mound, a suspected burial site. Are these singular stone markers some type of old property markers at both sites? Are they pieces of former foundations for old buildings? Or are they markers for alien burials? It is critical to note here that the last sentence of the old newspaper article gives support to the theory that Chapel One may have been the final resting place for someone, including the aliens. It states "There are stories of still another cemetery near the base chapel, but if so it's unrecorded." Hmmm, a widely known, undocumented burying ground possibly existing near Chapel One, recorded in a newspaper. Imagine that!

Ancient Burial Grounds on Wright-Patterson

"GLARC completed testing on 945.30 acres (of Wright-Patterson) and located seven prehistoric archaeological sites and 95 isolated finds." GLARC Report #389.

Wright-Patt Mound, aka *P Street Mound*, of the ancient Adena Culture.

Before we leave the topic of alien burial sites on the base, there is one other burial place that must be considered. Its location is geographically very close to the sites discussed previously, yet it is culturally and chronologically 3,000 years distant and makes for an interesting story...

Thousands of base personnel drive past two certified ancient Native American sites on Wright-Patt every day, oblivious to their existence despite the fact that one of these mounds is as obvious as a debunker at a UFO conference. Cleverly named the *P Street Mound*, after the road adjoining it, the obvious mound was the object of an extensive geophysical survey conducted in 1996.

The purpose of the survey was to use non-intrusive and non-destructive methods of examining an archeological site without the need for an excavation. Testing methods employed for the survey included Electromagnetic Conductivity, Electrical Resistivity Sounding, Electrical Resistivity Pseudosection, and Ground Penetrating Radar. Don't' feel bad about the techno speak, I'm not too familiar with these things myself and I have a Bachelor's of Electrical & Electronics Engineering.

According to the official survey report abstract "The geophysical surveys were successful at revealing some of the internal stratification of the mounds and also showed that there are unknown features, on or near the mounds." Further, these geophysical anomalies translate into "subsurface archeological features" 80% of the time when an excavation is performed.

This means that the geophysical survey participants believe there are archeological artifacts contained within the mound. A pre-survey document, The Ohio Archeological Survey form, specifies that human remains were previously extracted from this mound, bolstering the extended survey's claims.

I verified this fact with the Cultural Resources Office at Wright-Patterson and the aforementioned geophysical survey whose results were recorded in the book *Geophysical Surveys at Two Earthen Mound Sites at Wright-Patterson Air Force Base, Ohio, by Mark J. Lynott.* The book was written by the leader of the team that performed the survey on the P Street Mound.

The scientific fact that there are remains in the P Street Mound raises an interesting question.

Knowing that the mound would most likely never be disturbed – it is estimated that the mound dates back to the Adena culture and the year 1000 BC – would the caretakers of dead aliens be bold enough to bury them in the P Street Mound?

A strong argument in favor of the P Street Mound as a likely place to bury dead aliens on the base would be its high appropriateness as a location to conduct a Christian burial. This stems from the fact that in 1947 and thereafter, that site could have been an existing burial ground for almost 3000 years; there would have been deep historical precedence and thus easy justification to using this as an alien burial site.

If one were looking for the most symbolic of all possible burial sites on Wright-Patterson, the P Street Mound would be the best candidate. It would be a chance to reunite our unfortunate intergalactic visitors, who probably predate us by millions of years, with the oldest remains on the base.

Philosophy is nice but what does science say?

It is instructive to note here two very important scientific facts established at the P Street Mound that support a theory of alien burial at that location. First, there is conclusive evidence, via "magnetic survey traverses" that the mound was previously excavated "many decades ago." Secondly, conductivity tests at the P Street Mound indicate that are several "moderately large" (.5 meters) metal objects in the mound!!!

If there were no evidence of a previous man-made mound excavation disturbance then this site could pretty well be eliminated as a 1940's or thereafter alien burial site. But this is not the case.

And if the Adena people made copper ax heads .5 meters large we could speculate that's what being detected by the magnetic technology. But since copper ax heads are the largest metal objects they made and were never that size, we can rule out large ax heads as being the metal objects in the mound. Could these anomalies be alien caskets inserted vertically into the ground?

The strongest argument against using the P Street Mound would be answering to the authorities for the possible desecration of an ancient burial site and the lifetime *bad juju* curse that goes along with it. Then again, what lengths would you go to if it was your job to protect the most important secret of the millennium?

As we leave all the potential alien burial sites on WPAFB, it should be noted that the security forces' building is located very close to most of them. Patrolmen are always out and about, patrolling 24/7, even while the rest of the base is away and sleeping. As a consequence, security forces always have some interesting stories to tell, like the one that follows.

USAF Marathon runners patriotically glide past Wright-Patt Mound.

The story involves a world famous UFO abduction case and reminds us that just when you think you're absolutely positive about the people you should be able to trust most, you find out you could be absolutely positively wrong. It's especially unnerving when the "trusted people" are dressed in olive drab garb resembling military fatigue uniforms.

Everything on the Syfy Channel is not SciFi
– says former Wright-Patterson security forces member

I've spoken frequently to a retired Air Force member who spent their career as a security forces specialist, many of those years protecting some of the highest valued assets owned by the US Government. Coincidentally, they spent several of those years employed as security forces on Wright-Patterson.

One compelling conversation we had, amongst many interesting conversations, concerned my public questioning of long-time alien-contactee/abductee, Kim Carlsberg, who was a speaker at the 2014 IUFOC. Kim told the audience that in addition to her years of alien contact experiences she was abducted and interrogated by members of the US Military Services. Her evidence was a vivid description of the clothes worn by the abductors and seeing the posted military base-type signs as they drove into a fenced compound of ominous military-looking buildings. I pause to ask, "If she actually saw the military signs, what happened to the time-honored tradition of a black sack over the head of the abductee?" The answer is coming soon.

At the time of her presentation I completely and naively it turns out, pooh-pooed Kim's story because she claimed that although her abductors wore military-style uniforms, they did not wear nametags nor rank insignia. Since I had never seen a member of the military services in-uniform, without a name tag, that story just didn't compute with me at the time.

Weeks after the conference my former career-military source told me that while it would be extremely unlikely that actual active-duty military members would be the abductors, they were aware that civilian agencies have used military fatigues, of the kind Kim described, during the abduction and interrogation of US citizens! It was their confident opinion that usage of the pseudo-military garb and a convincing "military location" is just another element in a program of misdirection to undermine the witness's public story. After all, said my source, who could possibly believe that US armed forces would abduct a high-profile US citizen on US soil?

With respect to the usage of an "obvious" military base for the interrogation, my source explained that the US Government has numerous bases that are officially "closed" but whose mothballed facilities could indeed be used for purposes as Kim described. By allowing the abductee to see evidence of their arrival at a "military base" the abductors sell the idea that the "uniformed" perpetrators must be members of the US military. What other conclusion could a frightened abductee draw when all the evidence points in only one direction?

On the flip side, what if my source *is* aware of *actual* military abductions but is protecting their former comrades by creating plausible civilian-based scenarios. Hmmm. In this world one is never really sure.

In either case, the opinion of a singular former member of the armed services neither proves nor disproves Kim Carlsberg's claims, regardless of their occupational specialty or assignment locations. However, a person's opinion on any subject is more often than not a product of their cumulative experiences, either real or thru some common media. The fact is, uniformed military security specialists, like my source, are always creeping around an installation's high value assets while the rest of the population is away and sleeping; that's their job! Who better to know what we have and what we don't have, like abduction-ready buildings, since these nocturnal guardians can take undetected peeks around an installation without arousing suspicion?

A case in point occurred many years ago when some security forces at Wright-Patterson were stealing and reselling IBM Selectric typewriters from base buildings to supplement their income. Though they were eventually caught by more honest members of the force the point above is well established.

Based on their model patriotism, outstanding credentials and exemplary service record, I would have expected my source to vehemently deny any possibility that a US entity, military or civilian, would knowingly violate a citizen's rights in such an egregious fashion as Kim Carlsberg claims. But that didn't happen. Instead they named some well-known three letter agencies that they deemed are highly capable and, when properly motivated, are well equipped to perform acts that Ms. Carlsberg described from the podium at IUFOC 2014.

The unexpected news flash I was receiving from my source, that we could be abducting our own people, was the equivalent of the Pope himself whispering to me in a private Vatican conclave "there is no God."

Although extraordinarily rare, military security forces have been known to go in the wrong direction every now and then.

Upon lengthy and serious contemplation I can no longer ignore the ominous possibilities that my well-placed source and Ms. Carlsberg have laid out before me relative to her experiences. As a consequence, I tender my sincere and belated apologies to Ms. Carlsberg whose story now seems much more authentic due to my Wright-Patterson insider connection.

My critical acceptance of this dark news was hesitantly taken despite the absence of physical proof, alien or otherwise; it was time to move on to more Wright-Patt/Alien challenges.

The next challenge came in the form of two sunbaked, relentless, New Mexico-UFO researchers. These researchers were willing to provide the Air Force a once-in-a-lifetime opportunity to come clean about all things alien. Would the Air Force and could the Air Force take advantage of this golden opportunity?

Wright-Patt & The Plains of San Augustin Crash Material

"There's an old saying in Tennessee – I know it's in Texas, probably in Tennessee – that says, fool me once, shame on – shame on you. Fool me – you can't get fooled again!" President Bush, September 2002.

President Bush at Wright-Patterson Air Force Base, March 2008. Unsurprisingly, he did not say a single word about the base aliens.

A growing number of Roswell UFO crash researchers and theorists believe that more than one spaceship fell to Earth that early July 1947 evening in New Mexico. Some speculate that two craft were simultaneously subjected to the same navigational crippling force, possibly US radar, or lightning from a documented storm, or they may have crashed into each other; one falling close to Roswell, the other crashing on the Plains of San Augustin near Datil, New Mexico.

Principal proponents of the *Plains of San Augustin* crash theory are Art Campbell and Chuck Wade who have been researching that area for decades and have discovered some interesting material buried there in the New Mexico soil. That material has been extensively tested by independent labs using state-of-the-art analysis technology including scanning electron microscopes, energy dispersive X-Ray, Raman spectroscopy and Inductively Coupled Plasma Mass Spectroscopic analysis to name a few. These are words most people do not even know exist in the English language, so the equipment has to be impressive.

The results of those tests were reviewed by independent experts and the results were simple; simply out of this world. Phrases like "there is a probability that the material originated from a non-terrestrial source" and "may not have originated on Earth" are indicative that the material may actually be from a crashed alien craft.

In 2014 I was fortunate enough to meet the intellectually entertaining and refreshingly cantankerous, Art Campbell, at the International UFO Congress. As mentioned, Art and his partner Chuck Wade have been conducting alien archeology on the Plains of San Augustin in New Mexico for decades, reputedly uncovering material from an alien craft that crashed the same night as the Roswell event in July 1947. Perhaps because of my stated Wright-Patterson connection, what else could it have been, Art took me under his wing for a few days and we spent a lot of time going over his documented research.

After a week of casual negotiating, Art agreed to provide some of the metallic samples they collected to any reputable laboratory I could find to conduct additional testing and analysis. Although he was outwardly very excited when I proposed that these samples might be tested at the Air Force Research Laboratory (AFRL) Materials Directorate, I knew inwardly what he was thinking: "this guy is a few electrons short of a stable molecule."

What Art did not know is I had a plan in the back of my head; maybe not a foolproof plan but a plan nonetheless. I was planning on leveraging my association with current and former senior leadership at Wright-Patterson to get Art's recovered items retested in an Air Force lab. Yep, an Air Force lab whose owners wish to publicly stay as far away from UFOs as humanly possible.

Presented with a rare opportunity to expeditiously obtain and test scientifically verified exotic materials found in the desert, at a reputed alien crash site in New Mexico, what would the Air Force do? The obvious choices were: a) Provide excuses as to why they could not do such a thing, or b) Seize the day, test the material, and settle the debate for eternity?

At the 2014 International UFO Congress, Art Campbell provides personal tutorial on Plains of San Augustin UFO wreckage recovery.

I hereby readily admit that I was initially skeptical that they would carpe diem at all, but they surprised me. The reaction I received from AFRL's former leadership makes for an interesting Wright-Patterson true story which begins with the usual well-earned "there are no aliens" paranoia.

It's instructive at this juncture to illustrate how unbelievable my "test this alien material" proposition was to all concerned parties, myself included, by revisiting some additional Air Force and Wright-Patterson contentious UFO history.

To say that the US Air Force remains overly sensitive about the Roswell incident and anything UFO is equivalent to saying the Titanic sank; both are indisputable facts. Only one of these facts is mildly funny. You can decide which one after reading this section.

So concerned is the Air Force about the public perception of the Roswell incident, and the possibility of recovered alien artifacts in

1947, that in 1995 they published an explanation essentially denying an Air Force cover up. It consisted of nearly 1000 pages, as if any of the public was actually going to read *that*. Then, conspicuously near the 50th anniversary of the Roswell event in 1997, they published another 231 pages of explanation that mostly contradicted their previous tome.

Try to fool me twice, shame on you. My apologies to former President Bush who also regularly confounded the old adage about people who are less than truthful.

To be balanced and fair, let's look at my perception of the Air Force's unenviable position. Their main job is to keep the world's airspace safe and free from all enemies both foreign and domestic. It's a job they've done spectacularly well.

Then along comes a series of shiny airborne structural objects in 1947 that just won't go away. They are seen visually by the general population and military pilots alike, seen on radar – both ground and airborne – and can fly hundreds of times faster with more agility than anything the Air Force owns, including missiles.

It becomes clear to everyone, including the out-maneuvered Air Force, that it is impossible for the Air Force to do its job because it is faced with a problem it absolutely cannot solve in the near term. Every time one of these *objects* appears near a population center, the phone lines of the Air Force and local first responders, police, fire, etc. are jammed to the point where their operational efficiency is ground to a halt – a dangerous situation for the population. How does one pacify a concerned public that needs answers, and will concurrently return critical military and civilian defense operations to normal?

The Air Force's first "solution" was to tell the public that, yes indeed, there were objects sighted and the Air Force would handle the problem through Project Blue Book. When it became obvious to everyone that there was no solution because the objects just kept showing up all over the world, the Air Force used their variation of the old Jedi mind trick; "the objects you are seeing do not exist."

Although not much of a *real* solution, it did have the desired effect of turning off a good deal of public interest and virtually eliminating their pesky phone calls. Unbelievably, this is still somewhat the modus operandi of the Air Force to this day.

Today if you call the Air Force you will be told "we are no longer taking or investigating UFO reports." This is because they no longer have to in order to track the sightings or convince themselves this is not a temperature inversion, weather balloon, or twinkling stars. They only have to turn on the internet where they can find all the latest sightings and UFO reports recorded by Joe Citizen and the concerned UFO groups to which he belongs.

A huge public benefit of this new laissez-faire position is the Air Force has stopped insulting our intelligence with cockamamie stories like "several police officers were chasing the planet Venus." Thankfully they can give that steaming pile a rest.

But wait, all is not lost. There actually are some folks associated with the Air Force who really want to know what's going on up there with those shiny objects and are willing to take risks to find out. Could we overcome six decades of obfuscation and giggle factor and make a retest of the Plains crash material actually happen in an Air Force lab of all places?!? The answer may surprise you. But first, some essential background factoids.

While on a three year special assignment as the AFRL Wellness Leader I was a direct report to the AFRL Executive Director, a member of the Air Force's Senior Executive Service and AFRL's highest ranking civilian. The success or failure of my efforts on this special assignment could directly impact the current and future productivity of AFRL's entire workforce.

The results of my work were regularly reported to my boss and to the AFRL Corporate Board which consisted of every Director of every AFRL technical Directorate. At the annual AFRL Senior Leadership meetings, consisting of every manager across AFRL, my program was one of but a handful that was deemed important enough and corporately pervasive enough to be briefed to the entire assembly. All things considered, it was a high visibility/responsibility position. No brag, just fact.

As a result of the empirically measured success of my program, I had established a track record of sorts with my boss and AFRL's other top leaders. They knew me and I knew them, so my plan was to bring my alien material testing idea forward to some of those former leaders to see if they could make the necessary connections to get the job done in an AFRL lab. The worst they could say was, "Ray, *you* are a crazy son of a bitch!"

A former AFRL Executive Director, who declined to be named in this book, agreed to meet with me in his office to discuss "an item of mutual interest." At the time "Morley" was retired from civil service and serving in a leadership position at a notable Research and Development concern. I brought along a copy of Art Campbell's spiral bound book *Finding the UFO Crash at San Augustin; Isotopic Metal Analysis Not of This Earth.* In my opinion, this book provides scientific proof, via state-of-the-art testing processes, that some material recovered by Art Campbell and friends is of extraterrestrial origin. Repeat, not of this earth.

Could the former Executive Director and one of his most accomplished PhD buddies resist the opportunity to advance science for the benefit of all mankind? Turns out, they could not.

Morley listened intently as I recounted the Roswell and Plains of San Augustin scenarios; two alien craft that went down on the same evening in July 1947, perhaps as a result of a collision. One craft crashes 75 miles northwest of Roswell, near Corona, NM, while the other arrives 225 miles northwest of Roswell near Datil, NM.

The crash site closest to Roswell is picked clean of crash evidence by hundreds of available, conscripted military service personnel because of its close proximity to Roswell Army Air Field, later Roswell Air Force Base and then Walker AFB.

The Plains of San Augustin site is also discovered in a timely fashion but does not have a nearby military base from which to take day trips with large amounts of personnel to pick up the crash material. Because of that all the large pieces and aliens are recovered and the little pieces are either overlooked or bulldozed into the ground where they remained until Art Campbell and Chuck Wade arrive on the scene in 1994. Ooops!

As luck would have it, Morley would soon be meeting with one of the most accomplished PhD's to ever work at the Materials Directorate and would bring the material testing issue to his attention. In a few days, "Rusty", the PhD, proposes to another leading

172

scientist in the Materials Directorate that they test the Campbell/Wade desert findings, telling that scientist the initial tests suggest the material is from a crashed ET craft.

The fact that my seemingly outrageous idea, enlisting an Air Force lab to test suspected alien crash material, the Air Force's Kryptonite, got as far as it did proves only one thing which I always suspected, I wasn't the only "crazy UFO son of a bitch" in AFRL.

It is somewhat anticlimactic at this point to announce that "Harry", the decision maker we needed to get approval from, was not as enthusiastic about the opportunity to test the Campbell/Wade alien artifacts as Morley, Rusty and myself. Morley gave me Harry's bad, yet totally predictable news at a follow up meeting. The astonishing part of the reply was that Harry actually gave a plausible reason for not doing the testing rather than kicking his old co-workers directly to the curb.

Before the reveal, one must consider that this situation puts the US Air Force and the US Department of Defense in an unfortunate no-win situation. If they accept the material they implicitly say "there is the possibility that you did recover alien artifacts." This would put a huge dent in a 60+ year-old corporate position of denial. On the other hand, if they turn down the material with "you guys are crazy" they still look like the head-in-the-sand bad guys every UFO researcher believes that they are.

But shock, Harry did not turn down the opportunity by pointing his finger and saying "You crazy SOBs, we can't do that! You know the Air Force's position on all things UFO!"

Instead, we were unofficially-officially turned down because "the AFRL material testing pipeline is completely full for the next few years. Only government agencies with gobs of money will even be considered on a priority basis."

Unfortunately we were not a government agency and we had no money, therefore we had no chance. But we still received a calm and plausible Air Force rationale for being rejected; admittedly not a formal nor official rejection. This has to be considered an *unprecedented* position deviation, at least unofficially, after six decades of blindly denying the existence of anything in the air besides military and commercial air vehicles or the go-to answer to every unusual sighting ever, the weather balloon.

In case you missed the obvious, let me help you get your head around what just happened here.

One current and two former AFRL Senior Leaders, leadership at the highest possible level, seriously considered testing material they were told up-front was "not of this planet." And better yet, the materials were "the remains of a crashed extraterrestrial vehicle!" It's fitting here to pose a question Linda Moulton Howe once asked me "What's your Rorschach on this?"

If I were Harry, I would have taken some of the Wade/Campbell extraterrestrially-validated material in a heartbeat, and with no promises made, would have asked the author to sign a secrecy\non-disclosure agreement of some type. Since that didn't happen and only excuses were tendered by the active AFRL scientist, my Rorschach is they must already own some suspected or proven ET material and needed no more samples. The other option is, now that they know where to find ET material from San Augustin, they will get some directly from Art Campbell or Chuck Wade, with fewer people like myself in the loop to serve as potential witnesses to their curiosity.

Though I was unable in this instance to combine UFO peanut butter and chocolate together, all things considered, I have to ask you "Who wouldn't want to hang with great guys like the senior leaders in AFRL for four decades?" Especially when you can actually talk to them about aliens and crash wreckage reportedly brought to WPAFB in 1947 and not get immediately booted out the door. Then again, maybe it was just professional courtesy; an understanding that even suspected Men in Black can occasionally exhibit to other "government" employees.

Men in Black Encounter. Great Suit! Who's Your Tailor?

MiG Fighter adorns FTD (NASIC) at Wright-Patterson AFB.

It was Tuesday, 26 May 2015, approximately 0900 hours when I had my first and hopefully last encounter with The Men in Black. To be honest it was only a Man in Black, a singular male dressed precisely like one of the legendary UFO-witness intimidators. Black shoes, dark tie, lengthy black pants needing a tailor, black suit coat and black fedora hat.

What's so unusual about that outfit you might ask? This could have been just some ordinary guy taking a morning coffee break, dividing the monotony of just another day working for a top US intelligence agency. All things considered, I don't think so.

For starters my encounter materialized at the edge of the parking lot reserved for the Foreign Technology Division (FTD) on Wright-Patterson Air Force Base. FTD has been renamed NASIC (National Air and Space Intelligence Center), presumably to obscure its past as the home of Project Blue Book, but it's still referred to by locals in the know as "FTD."

On this gorgeous day I was playing the challenging Prairie Trace Golf Course which has property running parallel to the FTD complex. While on the course, my extra mission that day was to photograph the small cemetery located near the FTD parking lot for inclusion in this book. No one knew I was heading over to the course to play *and* photograph the graveyard.

Imagine my disbelief as I played my ball down the opportune side of the fairway, making a seamless approach to the gravesite, and then astonishingly encountering a man dressed as MIB. You could have knocked me over with a 4-iron!

I was so focused on spotting the rusted, wrought iron fence that surrounds the graveyard, my original objective, that I totally missed the MIB standing stealthily in the shadow of a large tree. As I gingerly approached the graveyard I eased my cart to a slow stop, making sure to keep the trees between myself and the all-seeing security cameras perched atop of FTD.

I gently applied the parking brake to suppress that loud clicking sound that golf carts notoriously produce. I furtively reached into the cart's cubby hole, extracting and concealing my cell phone in my hand. As I prepared for a careful exit, my eyes focusing on the graveyard, I heard a sudden voice from arrears.

Still not seeing anyone in the vicinity, including the MIB in the shadows, I was so stunned to hear a voice that it could well have been The Voice of God! This could be paybacks for the times I've inappropriately used his name while golfing I thought.

MIB: "Did you lose your ball?"

My head spun around 180 degrees to my left so fast I think I injured my neck. Standing under that shade tree, hidden so well by the shadows, was the MIB holding a large-sized smart phone encased in a dark blue shell. He was still looking down at its screen when I first made eye contact with his presence.

RS: "No, I didn't (lose the ball). I was just driving past and saw that fence there." (Pointing to the fence surrounding the graves.)

While I might have looked cool on the outside, this is what was going on inside just prior to my response:

"Holy shit! It's an MIB! And he's standing just yards from the legendary FTD building! Did he know I was coming over here to shoot the graveyard photo?! Impossible!"

Paranoia runs deep at times like these, my friend. To cover my distress I shot out a stimulating question of my own.

RS: "Is that a graveyard?"

Stupid question? Yes, but I just had to ask *any* question as a way of masking the fact that I'd seen this graveyard before and was there to take a photo on this particular visit.

MIB: "Yes, I believe it is." (Only looking up from his smart phone long enough to answer me, then right back to it.)

Sensing that this distracted MIB was more interested in his cell phone than me, I decided to forego the photo of the graveyard for the moment and slip out of the motorized cart.

RS: "That's really overgrown. You'd think they would take better care of a graveyard." (This is just one more undeniable piece of evidence of my brilliant conversational skills.)

MIB: "Now that it's summer I'm sure they'll cut it more often."

Is it just me, or does this initial exchange sound exactly like a Cold War-era, B-grade movie where two spies who don't know each other are meeting for the first time to trade brief cases after the obligatory exchange of cryptic password phrases? We had a graveyard. The only items lacking were a dense rolling fog and trench coats.

I walked over to the gravesite fence and positioned myself to read the headstones but was really getting a better view of my newly found friend. There was no doubt in my mind, if a convention of

MIBs were to gather on the spot, my friend would have blended right into the sinister crowd.

Since he did not seem overly interested in my activity, nor ask me any further questions, I relaxed a bit and returned to the golf cart without taking any photos.

At that point I SHOULD have hit the cart's accelerator and continued my round of golf. But, NO, my curiosity just could not let this opportunity to ask a few questions of my own pass so easily; I was about to walk that fine line that divides Einstein's genius from Christopher Titus's Inner Retard.

Addressing the MIB in a voice that made him momentarily abandon his smart phone addiction, he looked up in my direction. Then my inner retard took over full control of my brain and my mouth; he was unstoppable.

RS: "You know, given that we're in the shadow of the legendary FTD with its long history of UFO involvement, and the fact that it's 75 degrees out here with 80 percent humidity, and the way you're dressed with that suit, and especially that hat and all, I just can't help but think that you look exactly like one of those legendary Men in Black." (Yes, all in one breath.)

Let's pause here for the uninitiated. Men in Black are legendary guys who dress all in black; hats, suits, sunglasses, etc. They are accused of intimidating/abducting UFO/ET witnesses into silence/parts unknown and generally stealing, destroying, or obfuscating ANY evidence of a UFO/ET presence/encounter when they deem it necessary to do so. There are millions of words written about these never-photographed, shadowy, ominous folks elsewhere in the literature. If they exist they are usually portrayed as people you would rather not encounter.

At that moment I was thinking my encounter with this promising MIB could be UFO history. In all my years of UFO research I have never uncovered a single instance where the "witness" actually had the kahunas to call out the sveltely dressed gentlemen and insinuate that they were indeed MIB. Evidence of same may be out there, but I've honestly never seen it, presumably because the witness who finger-pointed and yelled "MIB!" was eventually whacked Tony Soprano style.

Apparently thinking that he could answer my rabid, ill-advised curiosity with a single gesture he did something totally unexpected. It was *just* the additional drama I needed at that cliff-hanging moment, another chilling revelation.

He switched the smart phone from his left hand into his right. Then using his left hand he removed his hat from his head and held the hat several inches away from his face. He then leaned forward towards me and tilted his head in a very subtle "ta da" motion, putting my squinting 20/20 vision to a serious test.

I could now see that his head was 100% devoid of any visible hair, he was totally bald or closely shaven. The skin tone of his scalp was the same as his face. And that's the scary part.

With the hat on, shadowing his face somewhat, MIB looked like a well-tanned professional golfer. Once the hat was removed, however, MIB looked a sickly "bone" color with an olive tinge. It just looked so unusual in the shadow of that tree!

Now I'm thinking, "OK, you took the hat off to show me you're bald to explain why you wear the hat. I get it. But that doesn't explain anything else, like why you're wearing that obvious costume just outside of FTD, a UFO Hall of Fame building if there ever was one, on a day that calls for Bermuda shorts and adult beverages with bright paper umbrellas?"

At that point I SHOULD have thanked him, hit the golf cart accelerator, rode off into the sunset, and blessed my lucky stars I was still a free man. But NO, I just had to dig deeper. Déjà vu anyone?

Most of us will pass this way only once. And, believing this is my one and only journey on this celestial plane I just had to ask the following question on this trip thru the cosmos.

RS: "So tell me, *are* you one of the Men in Black?!"

Shaking his head slowly from side to side, prior to and as he spoke, momentarily delaying his answer, I received a very soft, almost apologetic "No, I'm not."

I expected a quick "no." Or, "yes I am, and you are now really screwed." The total answer I received, replete with head motion, I need to run by behavioral experts to be 100% sure. But in the interim his answer has led me to conclude that he either was not being 100% truthful or he had taken high school drama classes; it was an effective display to further raising my paranoia.

At that point I SHOULD have thanked him, jumped on the golf cart accelerator, driven back to my car, packed my golf clubs in the trunk and found a safe hiding spot for the remainder of the week. But NO, I just had to ask ANOTHER question.

If I ever need to establish an insanity defense I'm going to copy these paragraphs and give them to the deciding judge. It will be a slam dunk!

RS: "If you're not one of the Men in Black do you mind if I take your picture?"

Someday, when Bruce Springsteen reads this book, and he will, he's going to rewrite his epic song *Rosalita* and replace a leading character therein named *Big Balls Billy* with my name. Mark that down.

Then, as smoothly and coolly as if I had asked for the time of day on the planet Venus, I received this response to my photo request.

MIB: "I don't think that's a good idea in this environment."

What the F@ck does that mean?! I'll tell you what that means; he let me off the hook. It had to be professional courtesy; much like a hungry patrolling ocean shark letting a vacationing, ocean-swimming Wall Street lawyer live for another day.

He caught me about to take photos with the FTD building in the background, a questionable deed at best. At the same time I called him out as a Man in Black. In his mind we played to a draw, nobody wins and nobody loses. Professional playground rules "No blood, no foul."

At that point I SHOULD have shut my mouth and gotten the hell out of there. And I did!

RS: "OK, I fully understand" (about not wanting me to take his picture.)

MIB: "Good. Thank you. Have a nice round (of golf)."

RS: "I will. Thanks. Bye."

MIB: "Bye."
And so it ended. Thirty minutes later, when I made my way around to that part of the course again as it looped back toward the clubhouse, I noticed MIB was gone. I exited my cart, went to the gravesite and took the photo undisturbed, making sure to keep the FTD building out of the frame.

I would be lying if I said that my paranoia quotient was not raised for the rest of the day, or week, or month. The conspiracy wired mind just cannot let something like this out-of-Hollywood encounter go easily into the night without a good amount of serious and well deserved contemplation.

So what really happened? There is any number of good possibilities; let's look at three.

Possibility Number One: About 20 minutes prior to the encounter I snapped a picture of a MiG fighter proudly displayed in front of the FTD building. Now hypothetically speaking, with the expected visual security around the premises it is most likely I was seen on a security camera performing this innocent act. In response, building security sent out plain clothes individuals to monitor my further activity as I progressed thru the golf course that borders the building. And I just happened to veer into the one security person who was dressed months early for Halloween in the MIB uniform du jour.

Possibility Number Two: There is some guy working in the former FTD building that gets his strange kicks dressing like the infamous MIB. He takes a morning break under the shade tree to review his personal email, which he cannot access inside the presumably shielded building, and takes great joy at freaking out innocent golfers on the adjoining golf course, sending them straight to therapy or writing UFO-related books like this.

Possibility Number Three: The dude was a real, live MIB. Hey, these guys have to be *somewhere* when they're not saving the free world, don't they? So why not have some of them hang out in *the* building that has always been closely associated with the UFO/ET phenomena that these guys reportedly protect?

Is there a better location for these boys to cool their black fedoras than one in which everyone is security vetted to the highest levels possible? I think not.

If I had met this guy in my favorite local restaurant or in the fitness center, I would have thought that some friends were setting me up for a joke because they are all aware of my interest in UFOs. But that wasn't the case. This happened in the shadow of *the one building* historically associated with the US Air Force's long running and self-documented UFO/ET connection. Coincidence or put on?

If my friends were responsible for pranking me they would have to know where I was going that morning and none did! And another thing, none of my friends are *that* resourceful.

For the record I shot an 84 that day, one of my best rounds ever on that golf course. Given a choice between my announced score that day and my MIB encounter story, my golfing buds would probably choose the "84" as the fiction part of the story. They'd say, "MIBs roaming WPAFB. Sure! Ray shooting mid-80's, sounds awfully sketchy to me!"

Could there also have been some unseen, cosmic influences at work on the golf course that day guiding my golf ball? Though I may never know the answer to that question, one thing is for sure, I promised to never let the MIB surprise me again. OK, never say "never."

The person dressed as an MIB was under the large tree about 15 feet right of the golf cart. The graveyard within the confines of this fence was featured previously in this chapter.

Stardate: 24 June 2015 - A Second Encounter

June 2015 had been unusually wet in Dayton, Ohio. According to the National Weather Service, rain levels were double the average of 3.63 inches per year. So it's no wonder that the golf course would eventually be packed on 24 June when the clear sky temps were in the 70's with very low humidity. Not wanting to miss this opportunity I cashed in a previously earned raincheck, Tom flipped me a key to a riding cart, and I was off!

It was just about 8:00 am and there was not a soul out in front of me for several holes. I reached the 10th hole along the border of the 800 series of buildings that comprise the former FTD, at about 0930. The 10th fairway is very narrow and I don't usually hit it down the middle of this intimidating expanse of green grass.

For some reason I was only thinking golf and nothing about another potential encounter with the Man in Black I had met one month ago just off this very fairway. When I arrived at my ball which I had unpredictably striped right down the middle, I got two surprises for the price of one.

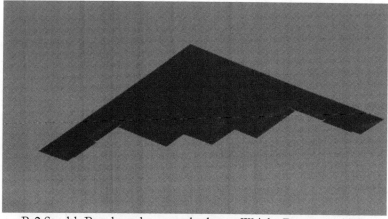

B-2 Stealth Bomber photographed over Wright-Patterson AFB.

First, a B-2 stealth bomber flew out right in front of me, apparently launching from the runway just a few hundred yards away. I suspected that it was on the base either for the recently completed Air Show or for the upcoming annual Military Tattoo. I wasn't sure which event was responsible for its presence but it was still totally unexpected; I should have seen that as an omen.

The B-2's sudden appearance as I started my way down the 10th fairway is probably the reason I was not even remotely thinking about another MIB encounter. By the time the B-2 bomber circled to the south and out of my sight behind the nearby trees I was near the FTD graveyard once again, exactly where I first saw the MIB one month ago. To my astonishment the MIB was back!

I should have freaked out. Instead, without hesitation and apparently without any common sense, I cut the cart's wheel sharply to the left and headed straight for him. I know what you're thinking; I must have lost my mind. Right now I can't disagree with you.

I stopped a polite ten feet away, much like one would do when picking up a playing partner who just completed their previous shot. Unlike what I would do to a playing partner, I did not jam the brakes on and intentionally drift the rear of the cart in their general direction, scaring the bejesus out of them; this was a moment for ultimate discretion.

My immediate conversation with the MIB went like this:

RS: "Hi, there."

MIB: "Hi."

RS: "You must come out here a lot?" (This was always successful in bars, so why not here?)

MIB: "Why's that?"

RS: "Well, every time I'm out playing golf you're out here."

MIB: "Maybe you play a lot of golf."

That's why MIBs are universally feared around the world, they're so clever and they know everything about you!

RS: "I'm retired now so I do play frequently, but I also run marathons and I'm writing a book and that's why I stopped over here."

I figure if you're dealing with a real live MIB it is good practice to impress them with the best part of your resume which can act as a magical shield against evil; somewhat akin to casual whistling while walking past a graveyard.

MIB: "You're writing a book?"

RS: "Yeah. Remember last time we talked and I asked to take your picture and you said 'not in this environment.' " (I was trying so hard at this juncture to suppress my inner retard.)

MIB: "Yeah, I remember. What's your book about, Wright-Patt?"

RS: "Wright-Patt will be in there. Some other UFO stuff too."

MIB: "Anything about Area 51?"

RS: "No, because I've never been there."

The guy is scary enough, dressed like MIB, standing in the shadows, and then he drops a very, very heavy one on me.

MIB: "I have (been to Area 51). You know you can get a guided tour of the place if you know the right people."

RS: "Can you?"

MIB: (Nods "Yes")

RS: "So do you (know the right people)?"

MIB: "Yes I do."

As we're talking I notice that he is wearing what looks to be the same suit and shoes as in the first encounter but the hat is different. It's a heavier material but in the same style.

I'm trying to stay calm but he's just told me he's had a guided tour of Area 51; no biggie, can't *everyone* have one?

After I collect my thoughts I really want to ask him about Area 51 but I want that photo more. (When serious UFO researchers read the previous sentence they will collectively try to have me committed to an asylum for passing on a chance to have an Area 51 discussion with a person who is likely an MIB.)

RS: "Well, you look so much like the mythological Men in Black that *your* photo, standing there with that graveyard in the background, would make an outstanding contribution to my chapter on Wright-Patterson." (I was looking at him with my arms extended, fingers upwards, and pointing my thumbs at each other in the classic pose of a person framing a picture with their hands.)

MIB: "I refused the picture because I don't believe any government employee whether working Intel (nods towards FTD building) or not should not be exposed on any type of social media. Know what I mean?"

RS: "Yes I do, but I wouldn't put it out there, only in my book with your face obscured." (I made a circular smearing motion with my hand.)

I'm sure he felt totally relieved about not being exposed in a book that could sell 20 copies or 20 million copies after I promised to perform a little Photo Paint magic on his face. Then he asked me another of the million dollar questions.

MIB: "Why would I let *you* put *my* photo in your book?"

RS: "Because no one has a clear picture of an MIB and one of those could make my book a best seller with you possibly getting a generous cut."

Did I really just say that?!?

There was a long silence, much like one the doctor makes before he tells you the results of an important medical procedure or biopsy test. Not wanting the conversation to end there, with the MIB slipping back into a smart phone induced coma, I caved.

RS: "You don't have to give me an answer right now. I'll give you my email address and if you want to talk more about this just drop me a note. I'm retired and can meet up to discuss it most any reasonable time."

Can you tell that I don't think things thru remarkably well under pressure? With that offer in the open he initialized the contact application on his smart phone, took my email address and asked for my name.

MIB: "What's your name?"

RS: "Ray."

Without my asking for his name he said: "I'm (name withheld)." Hey, I'm neither dumb enough nor brave enough to publish it.

RS: "Nice to meet you."

MIB: "So you're talking about a royalty?"

RS: "Yeah, something like that. Just get in touch with me if you have any questions."

I returned to my cart, hit the gas pedal and motored back to my ball. The MIB was still looking at his phone when I glanced over my shoulder. He was probably sending my email address directly to the National Security Agency, and every other concerned 3-letter agency, along with a photo of my inquisitive dead-man-walking face, just ahead of enjoying another healthy cigarette and quietly plotting my demise with his fellow MIB.

As I motored down the fairway on that sun drenched day, replaying the MIB encounter and discussion over and over again in my head, there were only couple of things I knew for sure. I do play a lot of golf *and* an authentic picture of Men in Black would make an *extraordinary* addition to a really good book.

Mistaken identity or the best MIB photo ever published?

While I cannot be 100% sure that this fellow is indeed a card-carrying member of the Men in Black he did drop a large number of excellent clues. First, he denied that he was MIB; always a dead giveaway of deception. Then he's dressed just like an MIB would dress, hat and all in the dead of summer. And finally, he's standing on the edge of a prominent intelligence agency property. At this juncture an old saying comes to mind "If it walks like a duck and talks like a duck, there's a good probability that it's a duck." In this case a duck dressed in MIB clothes.

ET Tries to Come Home to Wright-Patterson AFB

"We at the FBI do not have a sense of humor we're aware of." Agent K, *Men in Black* movie.

That same statement could be made by the Air Force in regards to anything associated with UFOs, ETs or off the planet unexplained phenomena. However, there was one very rare occasion where the Air Force was mildly amused with an unexpected UFO-related proposition that landed in their collective, usually protective laps.

I smile often when I think about the time I tried to introduce the entire Wright-Patterson population to the Roswell story, with the Air Force's permission, and nearly made it happen. Fortunately no aliens were harmed in the making of this all too true story of intrigue, deception and of course, the usual hijinks by UFO researchers and the humorless government alike.

An Alien Photo-Op was proposed for the Air Force Marathon Expo.

The story begins at the 2013 IUFOC (International UFO Congress) in Fountain Hills, Arizona, where I met Paul Davids for the first time. I do not recall how it happened, I'm just glad it did.

Paul is a very well-known writer of science-fiction films and "Star Wars" novels. He is a certified marvelous magician with a 25-year membership at Hollywood's Magic Castle. He has written, produced and/or directed a number of movies, the most important one of all to me is his Golden Globe nominated movie *Roswell*, for obvious reasons.

Sure, his is a great professional resume, but he also has the original four-foot tall audio-animatronic alien used in his movie in a display case in his home office. It stands there looking over his shoulder all day long as he works. It inspires sci-fi fans and creeps out all other visitors to his home; no surprise there.

After seeing his compelling *Roswell* movie and hearing about his alien office assistant I immediately began to think of them as my creative "peanut butter." All I had to do was find the appropriate "chocolate" and put them together long enough to make UFO history. Think "Reese's UFO Peanut Butter Cup."

A few weeks after our initial meeting I was back home trying to get my head around all the great people and presentations I had been privy to at my very first UFO conference, the one where I met Paul among many others. Maybe it was Paul's enthusiasm for the topic that inspired me, whatever it was I suddenly had a flash. How righteous would it be if Paul could bring his movie *Roswell* to the Wright-Patterson community for free showings?

It's been over 60 years since the Roswell crash incident; *surely* by now the Air Force had developed a sense of humor about the whole thing and could demonstrate same by supporting a movie show or two. I sensed a faint voice from the distant cosmos whispering in my ear, "Ray, you crazy son of a bitch."

I passed this whole Roswell-movie-on-the-base idea along to Paul who upped the ante by offering to bring with him the alien audio-animatronic model that appeared in the movie. We'd place this alien somewhere convenient so movie attendees could have a great photo op and long-lasting souvenir of Wright-Patterson's inescapable UFO legacy. All we needed was a venue somewhere on the base. It sounded simple enough but sometimes ancient history isn't kind to present day creativity.

To illustrate the risky creativity of bringing the *Roswell* movie and its alien to Wright-Patterson and to set the stage for the rest of the story, it's important to summarize the commonly accepted Roswell story and Paul Davids' movie treatment of it. For the uninitiated, the Roswell story itself is a simple one. What happened afterwards, for the next 67 years or so, is where it gets a bit complicated.

In July 1947, the Roswell Daily Record newspaper printed a story, submitted by the Army Air Force (precursor to current day Air Force) at Roswell (RAAF), proclaiming "RAAF Captures Flying Saucer on Ranch in Roswell Region." The very next day the AAF denied its own press release and have been denying and apparently obfuscating the original story ever since.

Meanwhile, UFO researchers have been gathering and collecting information refuting the AAF's (now Air Force) denials on Roswell for just about as long. Especially damaging to the official government version of the Roswell story is the testimony of one Major Jesse Marcel, the senior AAF intelligence officer stationed at Roswell when the event happened and the undisputed key witness to the whole mess.

Paul Davids' *Roswell* movie tells the story from the perspective of this Major Jesse Marcel who was sent to the debris field to follow up on a rancher's report and was of the opinion, in real life, that the crash debris "was nothing that came from Earth", and that the materials involved did not fit within his extensive knowledge base of known existing aviation materials.

Major Marcel was later ordered to pose for photographers with debris from a weather balloon, an obvious set-up so the Army Air Force could falsely claim Marcel made a mistake in identifying the material as a crashed alien craft; he unjustly suffered as the scapegoat the rest of his life.

In the *Roswell* movie, at an AAF reunion, Martin Sheen enters as Townsend, a character claiming to be the keeper of the Roswell secrets, and he dishes out the full array of the Roswell story to Jesse Marcel as having been mankind's first contact with alien technology. Although Marcel is never able to get solid proof from Townsend, and the movie ends with an unfulfilled Marcel staring out onto the field where he first touched the crash wreckage, the clear implication of the movie is the AAF hid something beginning in 1947 and has done a really good job of keeping it a secret. So much so that the very mention of Roswell tends to make the current day Air Force (split from the AAF in September 1947) do some very un-Air Force type things.

At this point it should be obvious to the casual observer that asking the Air Force to show the *Roswell* movie and its alien star on *the* base where Marcel claimed the crashed wreckage was delivered might be welcomed by the highly educated and entertainment-starved base tenants but not in a million years by the Roswell-besieged Air Force landlords. Can you say "Ballsy?"

While noshing around possible alternative movie venues, should the Air Force base have any surprising concerns about hosting, I contacted my good friend, Rob Aguiar, who just happens to be the director of the US Air Force Marathon. This event draws thousands of accomplished runners from all fifty states and beyond every September. The USAF Marathon office hosts a two-day Expo at the Wright State University Nutter Center and they are always looking for innovative ways to entertain Expo attendees.

When I proposed to the race director my idea to show the *Roswell* movie at the Expo and display the alien there as well, he said "What a great photo op for visitors to Wright-Patt!" Rob, obviously totally unaware of the Air Force's stressful public history with anything UFO, thought it was an absolutely inspired idea. Ahh, naivety, peanut butter, and chocolate, a perfect combination!

Rob the race director thought it was such a great idea that he even offered to pay Paul Davids' travel expenses and to pay for the shipping of the animatronic alien, IF he could get approval for same. I am 100% sure that he had *absolutely* no idea what he was about to be in the middle of, a classic public UFO interaction with the Air Force, essentially making us all "crazy sons of bitches." I couldn't have been prouder!

As you can imagine, Paul and I were absolutely giddy with the thought of potentially exposing the entire Wright-Patterson community to the Roswell story, four-foot tall alien and all, with Air Force approval and right in their own backyard. After decades of obfuscation, denial, foot-dragging, name calling, mind control experiments, media manipulation, and the most innocent act of all, outright lying, could it be possible that the Camelot moment was about to actually happen? It all seemed too good to be true.

Would Paul Davids and his Alien from the *Roswell* movie make it on time to the Air Force Marathon Expo at the Wright State University Nutter Center? Or would the 60-plus-year-old Air Force ban on all things Roswell continue? Note: Paul is the EBE (Earth Bound Entity) holding the magazine of choice for writers, movie producers and magicians alike, *Monsters*.

USAF Marathon Race Director, Rob Aguiar, on eve of 2015 race.

The first gauntlet we had to pass through was the Public Affairs (PA) Office of the 88th Air Base Wing (88th ABW) at Wright-Patterson. I was guided there by the former 88th ABW Vice Director, a man who was my supervisor while I was serving as the Director, Installation Civilian Wellness Program for the 88th ABW. This in turn put me in touch with Mr. Daryl Mayer, who at that time was the Public Affairs (PA) Operations Chief.

According to the Public Affairs Media Chief for Wright-Patterson, located in Air Force Material Command Headquarters, the purpose of PA is: "to communicate timely, accurate, and useful information about Air Force activities to DOD, Air Force, and domestic and international audiences. We provide trusted counsel to leaders; build, maintain, and strengthen Airman morale and readiness; enhance public trust and support; and achieve global influence and deterrence."

It may be useful to keep these words in the back of your head as you read the rest of the story. Then ask yourself if "the public's trust and support" was enhanced? I believe you will have a difficult time convincing yourself that actually transpired.

In the days following a lengthy phone conversation with Mr. Mayer, in which I described my objectives and answered his questions, I received the following email:

Ray,

I called the Air Force Entertainment Liaison Office about this request. They were not inclined to support. Your contact could contact them directly, if they would like an official response. There is actually a rather lengthy review process to receive official Air Force support including the rights to review the movie in advance.

http://www.airforcehollywood.af.mil/

You're kidding me, right? The US Air Force has a web link that appends the word "Hollywood" to "Air Force"?

I felt like Doc Emmett Brown in *Back to the Future* when he's told that Ronald Reagan is the US president and he responds *"Ronald Reagan?!? The actor?!? Then who's vice-president?!? Jerry Lewis?!?"*

Like Doc I found it difficult to take the PA office's answer seriously. My experience of working for the Wright-Patt base commander told me that if the Commander wanted to show a movie on their base (which was our Plan A) then by-God it would be shown on their base, Air Force Hollywood be damned. We will return to this fine yet extremely important point later.

Mr. Mayer, a very straight shooter, was kind enough to provide me the contact information for the Air Force Office of Public Affairs Entertainment Liaison (SAF/PACL) and I rang them up. I talked to Lt. Freeman who explained to me that she had discussed the issue at length with Mr. Mayer and had taken the request to the requisite higher authority within her office.

When I asked for a more formalized response than "no, you can't do that", she did have an answer that her "higher authority" had rendered. But it differed slightly from what she told Mr. Mayer, who of course had already shared the original response with me.

Lt. Freeman did offer me the following terse, somewhat robotic statement "It is not in the best interest of the Air Force." What she had told the PA Operations Chief, Mr. Mayer, was "SAF/PACL is not inclined to support the event as it presents material that is contrary to the Air Force's official position established in a prior publicly released report on the subject of the Roswell incident."

Maybe SAF/PACL felt that as a retiree I was not capable of processing the long answer either before or after my daily nap.

I also found the response to be very un-Air-Force-like because the two previous Air Force reports on Roswell have sufficiently been proven to be technically and chronologically implausible. The Air Force that bases current Roswell decisions on two highly suspect reports is not the Air Force for which I worked for nearly four decades.

Let's take pause for just a moment to entertain an interesting sidebar on the Lieutenant's extended quote above.

Let's agree for a moment that the Air Force lost all interest in UFOs in 1969 when they terminated Project Blue Book. That's what they said in 1969 and we believe it. They've only had to veer from that official position of disinterest twice. Both times to create and publish those aforementioned huge reports on Roswell, solely because of Congressional pressure and the need to do real Air Force work. Fair enough, they were momentarily forced to do it, and then they washed their hands again of the whole UFO matter; maybe not.

Given the Air Force's current public stance on the matter I had to ask "If they have no interest whatsoever on the UFO topic *how* do they *know* that the movie *Roswell* is 'contrary to the Air Force's official position'?!?" Was the movie title alone sufficient for them to create an official opinion on its contents?

That movie *could have been* an exposé on how a nefarious cartel of UFO researchers, led by Papa Stan Friedman, conspired to create a Roswell myth for the purpose of selling copious amounts books and putting paying meat in the UFO conference seats.

In that case the movie would have *supported* the Air Force's position. The only way they could know that the movie was "contrary" to their position is if someone in the chain of command had already reviewed the movie to be sure of its contents. And if they have no official interest in UFOs, as stated loudly since 1969, then why *officially* watch a movie about UFOs?

Methinks perhaps there are government job perks that the taxpayers are not yet fully aware of.

After SAF/PACL officially squashed hosting the movie on base, our Plan A, Plan B, show movie and alien model at Marathon Expo, went into full swing. The amazing thing was this switch-of-venue was done with the *tentative approval* of SAF/PACL; unbelievable!

Their totally unexpected reasoning was that the Expo would be held "off campus" and thus not subject to the review and approval processes for "on base" activities of this nature. They instructed that for off-campus events of this type only the base commander's approval would be needed for Plan B and "wished me luck."

You could have shot me off the Roswell roller coaster with a phasor beam. First, they say "hell no, not on base!" Then they turn around and casually remark "off base would be ok, with CC permission." What was going on here?

I was hopeful but exceedingly suspicious of the candy filled wooden horse they left outside my window, the one with the Greek graffiti all over it.

I immediately re-engaged with 88th ABW/PA to discuss this wonderful turn of events and they promised to investigate and advise accordingly. When Mr. Mayer subsequently contacted me with the news it was not so good. Despite an opportunity to make the Air Force Marathon Expo a memorable, one-of-a-kind, sensational event, Mr. Mayer did what many civil servants are trained to do, choose the most conservative path possible.

He told me he was not going to recommend that the base commander approve the event should I make a request directly to the commander's office at 88 ABW/CC. His rationale was that he had consulted with a peer who had previously handled "Roswell requests" and that peer went through "living hell" because they did not shut down the requests cold.

Subsequent conversations with Mr. Mayer and Lt. Freeman indicate that Mr. Mayer had a **lot** of help from higher authority in making his decision, although he and I were both assured by SAF/PACL that the decision would be solely in his hands (as recommending staffer) and in the hands of the base commander.

It is important to note here that all Air Force personnel I dealt with on this matter could not have been more accommodating, professional or forthright. Sure, the agonizingly legalistic corporate phraseology of their responses often made me want to scratch my fingernails on a blackboard just for relief. But there was no apparent foot dragging, no hiding of the organization chart, no subterfuge; it was all "this is the way it is so suck it up." And suck it up we did!

Perhaps the highly obvious, professional courtesy was tendered because I was once one of them, a high-level DOD employee for nearly four decades. Whatever the reason they didn't tell me to just shag off, it's that open communication with me that makes for such an interesting conclusion to this episode.

Perhaps feeling the need for a more experienced second opinion, the 88th ABW/PA office had a lengthy follow-up discussion with "Hollywood" SAF/PACL about the "off campus" Plan B. In turn, 88th ABW/PA admitted to me that 88th ABW/PA "based their decision of non-support mostly on the *guidance* they received from 'Hollywood' SAF/PACL."

At that point I should have grabbed my bat, taken my ball and gone home. But no, I had to find out why SAF/PACL would initially support an off campus viewing of the movie only to sabotage the only remaining chance I had. Surely Lt. Freeman could not have made this crucial decision on her own accord.

Four decades of civil service experience taught me that one has to reach the rank of Captain, as a minimum, before one can even begin to think nefarious thoughts, and must achieve the rank of Major or higher to actually act on those thoughts. So what really happened?

In a final "I should have known something was fishy by that smell in my nose" discussion with Lt. Freeman, she told me that her office is actually part of the Secretary of the Air Force's Public Affairs Office (SECAF/PA), the big dog of all Air Force PA offices. It is this office that sets the appropriate policy regarding UFOs and metes it out to organizationally subservient offices like SAF/PACL.

In a moment of totally unexpected and history making candor she told me that her boss ran my Plan B up the SECAF/PA flagpole for guidance from above. The "not in the best interest of the Air Force" response was what came down on the stone tablets from that mountain top. Actually, this is not too surprising and totally resonant with government policy to, when in doubt, CYA (cover your ass).

Further, she told me that indeed, the 88th ABW/PA office did discuss Plan B with her office and her office advised them of the current policy on such matters. When I reminded her that the Wright-Patterson base commander is *not* in her office's chain of command and her office should not be telling the base commander what to do, she replied "We do not tell base commanders what to do, we only *advise* them on current Air Force policy."

Fair enough, but when you preface your guidance to the commander's representative with "the policy covering that topic resides in the office of the Secretary of the Air Force" you are effectively removing the base commander from the decision making process, are you not? CYA, indeed!

As a sidebar, I used this "Word of God" methodology on a number of occasions while working for the Wright-Patt Base Commander (CC) when the power of my office was insufficient to conclude a critical task. A prime example was the reluctance of Base Civil Engineering to repair a broken blacktop walkway to be used for the CC-sponsored Wellness Walk. After I diplomatically advised the Civil Engineering Chief that the commander wanted it so, it miraculously was completed with due haste.

So, given the control that SECAF/PA apparently exercises over its satellite offices it is no surprise that the "local decision" was not in our favor; 88th ABW/PA effectively had no choice in the matter even though SAF/PACL told us it would be a local matter.

OK, so maybe SAF/PACL was just using a little sleight of hand here that Paul should have seen coming. Hey, he's the magician, not me!

In the end, Paul and I would be very disappointed at the missed opportunity but still maintained a sense of humor about the whole ordeal. At the 2015 IUFOC we had a short chat, filled with laughter, about how close we had come to actually pulling off what I consider to be the granddaddy of all military-related sleight of hands – something straight out of *Hogan's Heroes*.

Paul told me that he had recounted our story as a presenter at a large international UFO conference. A few months after IUFOC he repeated the story on radio shows, including a *Fade to Black* Jimmy Church show that had 150,000 listeners tweeting away their responses.

Like it or not, I guess I'm going to be a small part of UFO lore from this point forward. I'm OK with that. And with Paul being a certified marvelous magician and I still wanting to combine UFO peanut butter with UFO chocolate, who knows what our next exciting venture might be.

As a word of gentle advice to the US Air Force, heads up, stay vigilant, for there may be some UFOs right over your heads. In fact, in December 2011 that was the reality.

UFOs Flying Right Over Wright-Patterson

Thousands of UFOs are seen around the world every year. Many of those sightings are in the United States. So what's the big deal about a single sighting that took place in Ohio? Please allow me to enlighten you.

If my simple calculations are correct the UFO I observed for several seconds went directly over the main runway at Wright-Patterson Air Force Base just moments before I spotted it. Yep.

On Monday, 5 December 2011, I was oxymoronically driving southbound on North Fairfield Road in Beavercreek, Ohio, returning from a physical therapy appointment. As I departed the medical building where the therapy took place I immediately took notice of the very unusual weather that day.

It had rained sporadically throughout the morning, nothing unusual there. But by the time I turned onto North Fairfield around 11:40 am, following a forty five minute therapy session, the cloud ceiling was a super low sixty to seventy feet above the ground. It was at tree top level!

While I slowed my car down for the approaching red traffic light at Kemp Road I noticed a large airborne object pass from back to front through my peripheral view of the sun roof. Although the window of the sunroof was closed on this near 50 degree day, the sunroof blind was retracted.

This object was also heading southbound, about to enter the low cloud bank sitting immediately above the single-story buildings on the southwest corner of that intersection. As I applied the brakes even firmer I crouched down to look out the front windscreen and up in the direction I thought I'd find the object.

As I visually reengaged the craft, I was unsuccessfully trying to open the moon roof to my car for a clearer view. I kept blindly poking the ceiling with my index finger trying to engage the elusive button for the retractable window, not wanting to take my eyes off the fantastic object nor the cars that were stopping in front of me.

The very moment I was fully stopped at the light, the craft gracefully slid into the clouds and disappeared from sight. Replaying the entire event back in my head to estimate the total amount of time I had the craft in view, from first notice till disappearance, I would carefully estimate it to be about 7 to 8 seemingly slow motion seconds.

In the photograph below I've recreated the moment just before the craft went into the clouds. It shows the view I had relative to the craft and where my car was located relative to the actual street intersection which is shown in the photo.

I've enhanced the photo with my kindergarten-level rendering of the object at its location and height seen just prior to its disappearance into the clouds. I've never claimed to be much of an artist but the perimeter shape and roundish red lights were unforgettably distinguished. It convincingly reminded me of the trunk end of a 1960's era Chevy Impala, owned by just about everyone in Detroit, with its sets of triple cat-eyed tail lights on each side and the proportion of those lights to the entire visible back surface.

How strange is that? I wasn't thinking "holy shit there's a UFO!" Rather I was thinking "that UFO looks just like a Chevy!" I'm clearly a product of my environment and I tender that 9 out of 10 guys who grew up in my Detroit neighborhood would have thought the same about the craft's automotive-like design.

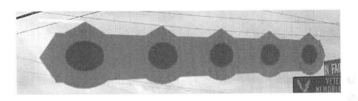

Top: Author's UFO drawing. Bottom: 1960's Chevy Impala.

The craft (added by author) was following a path parallel to North Fairfield Road, proceeding in a southerly direction as indicated. The craft was just above tree top level when the sighting occurred. The author immediately thought of a Chevy Impala with cat-eyed lights, an out-of-this-world ride in the 1960's.

Referencing the Google Earth image below, the red X indicates the location where the craft was observed as it headed southbound on a path parallel to N. Fairfield Road. If one draws a straight line from the X, in a direction consistent with the observed path of the craft, that line will pass right over the "freaking" center of the main runway at Wright-Patterson Air Force Base, a mere four miles away!

Admittedly I do not know the capabilities of the Wright-Patt radar. But I suspect that it might not have picked up an object that was cruising completely silent in the area, and only seventy five feet off the deck as this craft appeared to be. Certainly it would be spotted by the operational control personnel in the tower near the flight line, or would it?

I did not see any sense in contacting the base radar ops people or the local airport in Vandalia as I expected to get nothing in return for my inquiry other than denials, which may have been interesting in themselves. I do not recall hearing or seeing any helicopters or jet aircraft in the area after my sighting so it would appear as if the local US Air Force contingent only seconds away, had no knowledge of the intruder or had no available jets to chase it.

Either that or they had officially finally given up chasing objects they claim do not exist. It's about time.

This enhanced Google Earth Image includes the sighting location, large 'X', and a straight line extension backwards from there to where the craft was apparently approaching from, the main runway at Wright-Patterson Air Force Base. It is 4 miles from the Large 'X' at the intersection of N. Fairfield Road and Kemp Road, where I spotted the craft, to the main runway at Wright-Patterson.

The cloud ceiling on this day was unusually low which would have provided excellent cover for a craft capable of silently navigating less than one hundred feet off the deck. It is doubtful that the craft instantaneously appeared at the intersection where I saw it, unless its crew was craving fresh cake or sub sandwiches. Most likely it had been making a low-level recon pass over the area and would only have been exposed in the few available breaks in the cloud cover, just as I had witnessed.

When one considers the path I saw the craft on, it is not unreasonable to speculate that it had been on this path for a least a minute or so prior to my experience. If that was the case, and there is no reason to believe otherwise, the craft I saw could easily have passed right over the main runway at Wright-Patterson Air Force Base mere seconds before my sighting. Oh well, just another day in the Wright-Patterson neighborhood.

*   *   *   *   *

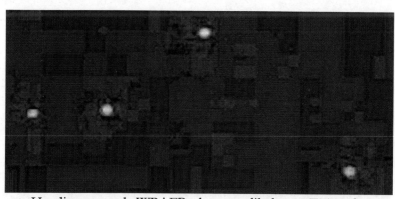

Heading towards WPAFB, these are likely not ET craft.

In November 2015, a formation of glowing objects was cell-phone videoed near the intersection of Fairgrounds Road and Beaver Valley Road in Beavercreek, Ohio. The three adult witnesses agreed that the objects were the size of a quarter held at arm's length and were completely silent. The sighting location is within three miles of Wright-Patterson, in whose direction the objects were travelling. Although an investigation by the author is ongoing, early research indicates these were Chinese lanterns. Other recent groups of similar glowing objects have been filmed and positively identified by eye-witnesses as lanterns that were on an almost exact route but much lower altitude as those pictured above. These lantern groups were *likely* launched from the same nearby location by the same individuals.

UFO Security Leaks at Wright-Patterson

"We're not hosting an intergalactic kegger down here." Rip Torn as Zed in *Men in Black*.

Maybe Zed was wrong.

The following story probably has absolutely nothing to do with aliens or UFOs at Wright-Patterson. OK, maybe it does. You decide.

Pictured below is the former Halfway House snack shack for Prairie Trace Golf Course on Wright-Patterson. In its heyday it served sandwiches, hot food and cold drinks to hungry golfers as they approached the halfway point on the golf course. Classified conversation was also apparently on its secret menu.

According to my source, a former long-term golf course employee, this hot dog haven also served as a lunchtime and break time gathering refuge for FTD employees. Yes, the FTD of Project Blue Book fame.

Though the Project Blue Book organization has long since renamed itself NASIC (National Air and Space Intelligence Center), it's still referred to as FTD by a majority of the current base population. Because this snack shack is a mere two hundred yards from FTD it was a convenient place for FTD'ers to grab a hot dog and beer and catch a little ultraviolet light that is so hard to come by in the virtually windowless FTD building. It was also a good location to socialize with fellow employees outside of their notoriously restrictive, focus-demanding venue.

With food, sunshine, friends from work, good conversation, and beer all readily available what could possibly go wrong here? The correct answer is, all the above.

According to my highly placed source, some employees from FTD were overheard or observed discussing their projects at the snack shack during their lunches, after work and during other daily breaks. Apparently there was a good deal of beer consumed, in addition to right-priced food, which helped FTD employees really unwind when necessary. What's worse, if this could get any worse, is that *anyone* on the base could have taken a seat at the snack shack to

207

overhear any and all of these conversations; this includes thousands of base employees with clearances far below those carried by the careless conversationalists!

This convenient golf course Halfway House was home to many FTD employee lunch and ultraviolet breaks until leaks were suspected.

Once the problem of inadvertent disclosure risk was brought to the attention of the appropriate base authorities it did not take long for the snack shack to be scheduled for permanent closure. During the closure transition period, my personal discussions with soon-to-be-former snack shack employees made it clear that they were told the closing was due to the snack shack being a "money losing venture."

One Halfway House employee voiced their disbelief to me of the official explanation, a disbelief that was based on their personal knowledge of how much money the venture was actually making. But by then the closure decision had already been made and was deemed not debatable by the base authorities.

In a worst case scenario, if Wright-Patterson's FTD employees were discussing actual alien projects at the snack shack, who might have heard these discussions and what did those people do with this newfound knowledge? Does anybody know what damage was done, if any, to our national security at this location? Was anyone censured for this apparent breach of security? This sounds like a new string of Wright-Patterson UFO mysteries waiting to be investigated.

The only thing for certain in this documented case of highly effective "beer counter intelligence", pun intended, is "loose lips, lose their beer privileges" or something like that.

Wright-Patterson's UFO Culture Updated: 2015

Not much has changed at Wright-Patterson relative to the "aliens in the tunnels" thing I first heard about over forty years ago. Not only are the younger employees still being indoctrinated in Wright-Patt alien lore but the base community also finds regular opportunities to crank up the alien giggle factor and publicly maintain the Air Force position on all things ET – they don't exist. And they are getting so clever about it!

On 21 August 2015, I had a conversation with a young NASIC (nee FTD) employee regarding their exposure to the UFO/ET topic at work through their fellow employees. They related to me that during a recent problem with the NASIC building air handlers creating noticeable noise in the walls, the employees were all joking it was caused by aliens trapped in the building. They also related to me that during their first few weeks in the NASIC building they were told matter-of-factly that the rumors of aliens in the basement were true and were let in on the "secret" because no one would believe them anyway. Upon hearing this I began to have another serious case of déjà vu, a phenomena I experience every September at the Air Force Marathon.

For the past several years I've served as a photographer for the Air Force Marathon, being one of only a few official motorized photographers allowed on-course for the race itself. This privilege provides me a unique opportunity to photograph all the hard working race volunteers, including those manning the NASIC hydration station whose volunteers distribute water and Gatorade to the runners, miles away from the finish line.

While other hydration station themes tout swashbuckling pirates, gyrating Elvis wannabees and swing dancers, NASIC consistently plays up their alien heritage with brilliant ET costumes and UFOs of all sizes. If given a choice I'm sure they'd substitute oozing green slime for the Lime Gatorade they generously dole out to thousands of the perspiring runners.

Other running events on the base get into the alien act by using the Extraterrestrial theme on the actual event t-shirts. In 2015 the 88TH Force Support Squadron/WP Fitness Program's Half-Marathon race shirts, procured by race coordinator Mr. "Taz" Petersen, featured two aliens and a classic disc-shaped craft. Since the vast majority of the fitness program employees were not even born when *Project Blue Book* closed its pages, one has to wonder how these young employees made the connection between UFOs and Wright-Patterson. Could it be that the Wright-Patt System/Network, described earlier, is still going strong to support this cultural history?

An escaped NASIC Alien cheers on runners at the 2014 Air Force Marathon run on Wright-Patterson. NASIC is the former FTD.

*   *   *   *   *

One of the last places I expected the alien giggle factor to be elevated is The National Museum of the United States Air Force at Wright-Patterson. This spectacular institution has over 1 million square feet of exhibit space honoring the Air Force's proud past. Even with that mind boggling amount of floor space the National Museum is only capable of displaying a small fraction of its entire holdings, with the remainder in local warehouses and at a large number of geographically dispersed sites.

One of the local warehouses is Building 5 at Wright-Patterson in Area B. Upon entering the building one is instantly reminded of the famous closing scene in *Raiders of the Lost Ark* where the crated

Ark is casually placed next to one of millions of other similarly marked and crated items.

Likewise, Building 5 contains a seemingly endless array of aeronautical treasures like a full cockpit mockup, F-117 Stealth Fighter flight simulator. But the interior similarity of Building 5 to the Ark's final resting place is not the only subtle and possibly accidental giggle factor at play here.

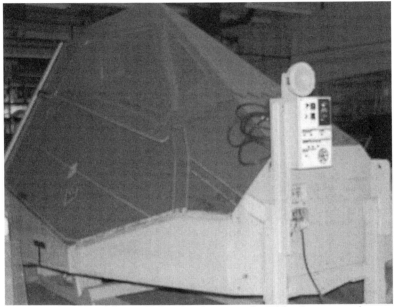

F-117 Stealth Fighter Flight Simulator awaits Bldg. 5 repurposing.

Proudly displayed at the entrance to this mega history stronghold is a sign declaring that the entrance is none other than Door 18. I know, it doesn't say "Hangar 18", the mythological delivery point for the 1947 Roswell crash wreckage, but when one considers that very few buildings at Wright-Patt have door number signage it would appear that humorous homage is clearly being paid to Hangar 18. And behind nearby Door 17 it's possible you'll laugh aloud, too, at the Air Force's present day "underestimation" of the public's ability to recognize a steaming pile of bull. Or maybe it's just a test of our sense of humor.

The National Museum of the United States Air Force maintains a Research Division which owns a small amount of interesting physical and written material bequeathed to it by the Aerial Phenomena Office of the former Foreign Technology Division (yes, *that* FTD) and other sources. One gains entrance to this exotic space-wannabee material through Door 17 and an appointment.

I suppose if this FTD-sourced "spaceship'" material was recovered in 1947 some of it would require about ten minutes investigation to determine exactly what they were dealing with. The remainder of the objects I viewed are so obviously not a piece of a spaceship that I couldn't help but laugh out loud myself.

Perhaps my spontaneous laughter outburst was a bit immature. After all, the aliens could have found good use for the roached-out, name brand, Ray-O-Vac batteries that were embedded in one of the suspected spacecraft artifacts presented to me by the clearly embarrassed Research Division staff. And since the artifacts were released by the former FTD, did I *really* expect that any of the good stuff – the authentic artifacts - would find its way to the light of day. Of course not! It's not the planet Venus, but it is an entertaining pile of hooey they let me examine.

If you ask me what I think, and I know you do, I believe this material was preserved and released to the public for the purpose of official disinformation. What FTD said years ago, and the museum is now saying is "look at this obvious terrestrial material brought in for analysis by those who *believed* it might be part of an alien spacecraft. It just goes to show you how easily true believers are fooled into thinking that something very ordinary could be extraterrestrial." Wow, I'm so fooled!

To this President Bush would say, "Please don't try to fool me again", or something like that. And I agree. I honestly cannot believe that anyone would turn in a package containing common batteries and claim they were extraterrestrial. What is even more unbelievable today is the US Air Force wants us to believe that there was a US citizen stupid enough to make that contention, current reality TV shows notwithstanding. The US Air Force always amazes me, in ways both good and not so good.

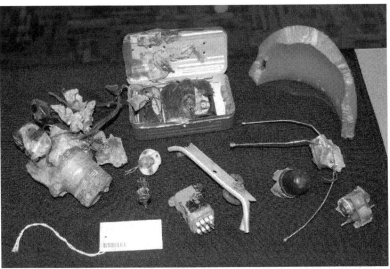

If we believe the US Air Force, US citizens apparently thought extraterrestrials were using Ray-O-Vac batteries to power-up components of their intergalactic spaceships, repurposing my 4th-grade lunch box in the process. Mercifully they hid the Fruit Loop reactors.

$*$ $*$ $*$ $*$

Many former and current Wright-Patterson employees who contributed to the material in this book have graciously asked that they remain anonymous. Although a story seems more authentic when it can be connected to a named principle character, and the readers deserve the same privilege, legal considerations leave no choice in the matter. That said, I assure you that I have faithfully passed on to the reader as many details as possible from the original sources.

One former Senior Executive Service member whose story appears in the book informed me in a phone conversation that "SES's never really retire" and must uphold the same Air Force standards that they did when they were full time employees. Since the Air Force's official position is somewhat contrary to the information that the SES shared with me, any reticence to be publicly identified is easily understood though reluctantly accepted.

It is also important to understand that much of the information sourced to me and contained in this book was provided to me as a "trusted fellow insider", given to me prior to the onset of writing this book. I'm fairly certain that if I had asked fellow insiders for the same information, with the announcement that it was to be published in a book, I would have been denied out of their loyalty to and respect for the Air Force. And quite frankly, had I known "a priori" that I would include the provided information in the book, I probably would not have placed some of my sources in what is proving to be an uncomfortable position, for them.

There is no doubt that many important current and former Wright-Patterson employees are still concerned about being connected to the UFO phenomena in 2015. Fortunately for these sources I would never abdicate their trust, or that of any future sources. Hopefully I have sufficiently masked the identities of those asking to remain anonymous. Should any of you be asked, may I suggest "deny, deny, deny" – it would not be an unprecedented UFO-situation strategy.

Chapter Epilogues

Finding the Truth about Wright-Patterson's Mounds

A representative from the Wright-Patterson Cultural Resources Office (CRO) met with me at the site near the Foulois House that holds a small mound and flat stone marker. In the main body of the chapter I suggested that it was a possible alien burial site.

After visually inspecting the site the representative posited that the stone was concrete in nature and was most likely a leftover cornerstone from former buildings in the area. They could not explain the mound itself and suggested it was merely buried rubble.

Though it is entirely possible the mound I discovered *is* buried rubble, it is unlikely that the stone marker is part of a building foundation. A review of base maps beginning in 1947 does not show any building on that site which would have left a cornerstone or foundation fragment once a building was removed. Someone will have to show me a photo or a useful map with a building on that site to convince me the stone is part of an old man-made structure.

When I suggested to the CRO that they excavate the site to determine exactly what its contents are or are not I was told that a complete study of the base archeology was in the planning stages. I will be following this as close as possible and hopefully reporting on it in my next book.

It is not unusual to find a few random small mounds here and there around Wright-Patterson Air Force Base, like the one I discovered near the Foulois House. And although they may be small mounds some of them have been found to contain big surprises. Take for instance the Twin Base Golf Course Mounds which unfortunately for base authorities were not an ancient Adena burial site.

In the mid 1970's the Environmental Protection Agency became aware of some unusual earthen mounds that surrounded the Par 3, Number 4 hole on Twin Base Golf Course. We golfers thought the design was a nod to the Scottish heritage of the game whose links courses are strewn with smallish bumps and mounds; meanwhile the EPA was not amused by the course architecture or its contents.

Shortly after the EPA investigation and excavation began on those 'links-type mounds' it was determined that the barrels unearthed from underneath those stylish mounds contained a variety of toxic chemicals. This might explain the five-legged deer that was often seen in the area during this period and the four-foot tall bunny rabbits.

In a discussion I had with the Twin Base head golf professional during this stretch, Bill Kumle, he told me he was spending more time with the EPA sorting out the buried chemicals on his golf course than he was helping customers in the pro shop. These mounds proved to be just the proverbial tip of the iceberg as far as buried toxic chemicals and other dangerous stuff uncovered by the EPA at Wright-Patterson; a pattern that repeated itself everywhere on the base whenever the EPA was looking for work to do.

Did I mention the ninety-two, 1950's-era germ-warfare bomblets that were uncovered when the contractor broke ground for a new fire station water line on Loop Road in Area B, just across the street from Building 620? Or the thousands of gallons of jet fuel poured directly into the ground in Area B that took years to remediate? Or the nasty stuff they found around base housing that caused them to destroy entire housing plats on the base and fully remediate those areas too? Need I say more about buried objects?

At this point there is only one conclusion that I can draw. If we consider the long and proven history of Wright-Patterson tenets burying everything under the sun on the base, perhaps it's not a long stretch of the imagination to think that a few cubic feet of Wright-Patterson Air Force Base soil was used to give unlucky extraterrestrial visitors a proper burial when the time was appropriate.

My only foreseeable regret of retiring early is missing a chance to see the EPA inspector's face when she uncovers *that* little treasure trove.

A singular stone marker, the same relative size and shape as those discovered at the FTD cemetery and the undocumented Skeel Avenue mound discussed prior, also appears at the base of the plateau upon which the Wright-Patt Mound rests. Is this a coincidence or a purposeful pointer?

Roswell is Dead, Long Live Roswell!

"It's kind of fun to do the impossible." Walt Disney

Roswell is synonymous with UFOs and Extraterrestrials because we've had nearly 70 years to make that association happen. There are countless well-researched books, movies, TV shows and documentaries recounting the time-worn Roswell story. There are also well designed museums dedicated to its memory. But after all these years invested by serious researchers, enthusiasts and those just looking to make a living, and after all this documentation generation, there is one thing that is as inescapable as death and taxes – not a single shred of immutable scientific "proof" has ever been produced to verify a UFO crashed and was recovered in 1947. Not a single molecule.

What we do have after all this time is nothing but a mountain of words. Words spoken as untimely death bed confessions by those who claimed to have been there. Words on sealed affidavits opened only after the death of purported witnesses. Words spoken to researchers by self-proclaimed witnesses whose veracity has often come under fire – both the veracity of the witnesses and the researchers!

There are "authentic" government documents, located in archives by reputable researchers that record the military's opinion that "the phenomena are real and not visionary." These authentic papers are supplemented by unverified secret government documents that were anonymously sent to reputable researchers whose associates have supposedly validated their authenticity without anything but a photo copy of the document in question because the originals film negatives would not be made available by the owners. Phew! It's enough to make even the staunchest Roswell believer take an interest in anything but UFOs and move on with their lives because the debate about UFO reality is both dizzily circular and endlessly contentious – even amongst friends.

If you are looking for some factual full disclosure, here's some for your consideration. I have read dozens of books on Roswell and related phenomena, watched the movies, TV shows, and documentaries. I've read hundreds of pages of web-based content on the subject. Through all of this I did not see one photograph of an alien, a spaceship or piece of metal that convinced me that any of it is real proof of an alien crash in 1947. For now, the best evidence we currently know of can be reviewed in *Finding the UFO Crash at San Augustin* by Art Campbell.

An extensive presentation of *Finding the UFO Crash at San Augustin* is unfortunately well beyond the scope of this book. That said, with few other exceptions like Dr. Roger Leir's book *Alien Implants*, there is very little hard scientific evidence publicly available with respect to UFOs and Extraterrestrials. In Campbell's book, state-of-the-art high-tech laboratory equipment is used to reveal that metallic material recovered on the Plains of San Augustin, by Campbell and his associates, is most likely extraterrestrial. Commenting on a recovered sample whose isotopic ratios were scientifically measured (how else?), the book's materials-science scientific consultant states "there is, therefore a high probability that **the samples came from an extraterrestrial source**." (Bolding is Campbell's in his book.)

In addition to the compelling summary of scientific observations and conclusions presented in *Finding* there exists a 42-page full report on the testing accomplished up to the point of the book's publication that is available for review. This is a refreshing change from all the skullduggery, secret documents and conspiracies that have plagued Ufology from the very beginning. But this may pose a problem for those who hold the sacred mantra "it could only happen at Roswell." Could the scientific evidence contained in *Finding* be the end of the long-running Roswell cash cow, and/or the beginning of a new Gold Rush on The Plains of San Augustin?

If the UFO community is *really* interested in proving the existence of Extraterrestrials and their spacecraft or disproving yet another wild rumor spawned in the New Mexico desert, this time near San Augustin, there is an easy way to do it. I propose we take a community collection and fund a complete set of scientific tests on materials collected by Art Campbell and associates. Then, carefully create a panel of scientifically qualified individuals to select the testing laboratory, monitor the process, and distribute the results to everyone – whatever those results may be.

If the results show that the materials are definitely of this planet, then another good myth is put to a long-overdue death. But if the results are inconclusive or determined to be definitely extraterrestrial, then the community needs to expeditiously organize a great big archeological safari with proven experts, go out to San Augustin and collect every last spec of material evidence before it falls prey to those who would like to keep this story untold.

If the San Augustin artifacts are proven genuinely extraterrestrial, the benefits to the UFO community will be life changing for the brave who dared to be involved with this story anywhere along the timeline. If the materials are proven genuine then those researchers who inflated their college credentials to elevate their status as an investigator or witnesses who altered their telephone bills in an act of revenge could be instantly forgiven – because those indiscretions will no longer matter!

As for those who make their living off of the Roswell story all is not lost. They can revisit all the old theories of what might have caused that crash and update those theories to include the newly validated crash site. This geographical expansion of the original event will force researchers to re-evaluate the entire story, to look into new locations and to closely examine the movements of all key military individuals at the time of the crashes, not just the military in and around Roswell. A whole new industry will be born. Then, and only then, I suggest building the best UFO museum ever constructed and place it smack dab on the actual Plains of San Augustin crash site and say "We told you so!"

If you prove it's real, they will come.

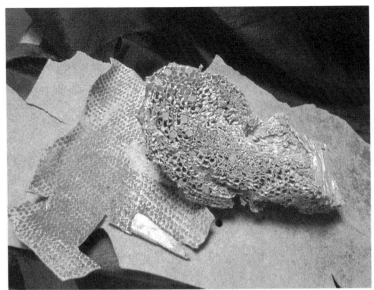

Artifact recovered in 2011 on the Plains of San Augustin. The honeycombed material is extremely lightweight and was found with what appears to be a matching skin that has a corresponding honeycomb pattern clearly seen in the photo. The straight line cuts resulted from material being removed for testing.

Ever the history teacher, Art requested that his archeological partner in his two decade long adventure, Mr. Chuck Wade, be given equal if not greater credit for all the discoveries that were made on the Plains of San Augustin. He also wanted me to note the significant contributions of chemist and material scientist, Mr. Steve Colbern, and those of Mr. Gerald Anderson, of whom Art said "It was he (Gerald) that brought into daylight the long buried debris."

Consider it done.

The Great Roswell Caper: Foiled Again by the US Air Force

There is no doubt in my mind that the Wright-Patterson population would have loved Paul Davids and his audio-Animatronic Alien as a US Air Force Marathon Expo photo opportunity. What I did not know until we had our plan squashed by the powers in Washington was Paul had decided *not* to fly himself and "Al" to Dayton. Rather he had decided he would take his sweet time getting there by driving both of them cross country. In the process he was going to make a documentary of not only the public's reaction to "Al" on the drive but also the fan reaction at the Expo!

Paul Davids readies for a cross country trip with his ET pal.

Paul had scripted out in his fertile imagination a humorous scenario where he is pulled over by the unsuspecting police for a minor speeding infraction, a petty crime he was willing to commit for the sake of the documentary. The objective was to film the officer's reaction while the officer evaluated Al sitting in the front seat and Paul laying it on thick about his galactic hitchhiker. These are the type of video moments that go net viral in days while the police officer deflects the "he's cuckoo" looks from everyone else in the precinct.

Maybe we'll get it next time, Paul. There's always a next time.

UFOs over Wright-Patterson and The Oz Factor

If someone sees an unusual airborne object it is usually best to record the sighting as soon as possible afterwards to guard against typical human memory fading. Despite holding this advice near as one of my personal mantras, I did not fully record my 5 December 2011 sighting upon arriving home from a physical therapy appointment. In fact, I did not actually sit down to sketch a more detailed representation of the craft I saw that day until almost exactly six months later.

I had many more medical appointments in the months following my sighting that required me to drive past the sighting intersection. Each time I did so it would trigger a reminder of my sighting and I'd say to myself "I need to write everything down about that day."

But lo and behold I would arrive back home only minutes later and totally not write anything substantial down on paper! It was as if there was some dark force in the universe that just would not let me accomplish that very simple task of fully sketching the craft and filling out a sighting form.

This unexplainable aversion to recording my sighting's factoids is even more mysterious given that I am addicted to note writing, a skill I perfected during my decades as an engineer. I have dozens of full notebooks to verify this consistent behavior.

The most plausible explanation for me, of my inability to record my sighting, is what some researchers have termed the "The Oz Factor." In its most obvious form, individuals having a close encounter with an alien craft and/or its occupants describe a "time standing still" effect; no sound of any kind and everything moves in slow motion. Their memories are repressed and can only be brought forward from the subconscious to the conscious through hypnotic regression or a long passage of time and a trigger.

If memory losses or blocks can be induced by alien craft, as attested to by multiple documented cases, then it is possible that those of us who were in the craft's immediate vicinity on 5 December 2011 fell victim to this capability. But just how did I snap out of it?

To be honest, I'm not exactly sure how the mental block was removed that was keeping me from recording my sighting, but I did discover something interesting that happened on the day I finally sketched out the craft on 6 June 2012.

On that day I received an email from the contractors who were working on my final project just before I retired in September 2011. The project continued after my retirement, proving once again that everyone is replaceable, even veteran engineers with a penchant for UFOs.

After responding to the question posed in the contractor's email, I drifted into a long mental retrospective on my lengthy professional career, up to and including my car accident – the reason for my retirement – and the required physical therapy. It was at that moment the image of the craft came back clearly into view and I drew it out.

Perhaps it was my thoughts of an unfinished career that were in the way and when I finally came to terms with that, and dumped them from my memory, I could once again clearly see the craft and remember all the details. I do not know for sure. Maybe there is a psychologist out there with the proper experience and credentials who would like to weigh in on this. I'll leave it to these experts to ponder this strange mystery.

Where did all the really cool FTD shit go?

In 1970, the year after Project Blue Book staffers took their Buck Rodgers guns and went home for the final time, FTD donated several items to the Air Force Museum at Wright-Patterson. Those items were initially collected by FTD apparently because each accompanying story made it plausible that the item had arrived from outer space, either man-made or not.

Found in 1957 Tiffin, Ohio and ruled a hoax by Blue Book's lab partners.

Dutifully, FTD had each item evaluated by a cooperating laboratory and each item was eventually dismissed as intentional hoaxes or naturally occurring earth items, sometimes developing under unusual circumstances like a downed power line.

It would be spectacularly naïve to conclude that FTD collected only this handful of items to evaluate during its nearly thirty years of UFO investigations. This begs the obvious question: Where is all the other physical "stuff" that FTD collected over all those years?

Everyone knows that the Project Blue Book case files are at the National Archives. Check! But there could be thousands of other physical trinkets out there that were turned in to Blue Book by honest, though often technically undereducated American citizens. After all, America is still mostly farmland, not tech labs.

According to the National Museum of the US Air Force Research Division (formerly The Air Force Museum) it is their understanding that "any Project Blue Book material generated or collected by the project, and not deposited in the National Archives, was destroyed. **Further, there is no record available of the actual**

disposition of these (invaluable) artifacts." By their own admission they have no concrete information on the final disposition. Another clear case of you don't know what you have until it's gone. "Invaluable" added by author, above.

Undoubtedly 99% of this stuff would have a prosaic explanation, but some could have been evaluated to be of non-terrestrial origin. Where could these 1% items possibly be stored?

Maybe all the smaller, real pieces of extraterrestrial material are in office file cabinets just like Lt. Col. Corso claims in his book *The Day After Roswell*; wouldn't surprise me one bit.

As far as Senator Barry Goldwater is concerned, his well-known public pronouncements clearly indicate that he did not gain access to FTD's Blue Room, reputedly the Holy Grail of recovered alien crash wreckage. However, a long time FTD employee did relate to me that they saw Senator Goldwater with their very own eyes moving through the hallways of FTD on crutches during his visit there in the early 70's. Perhaps Goldwater got closer to that special room, if it exists, than he was willing to admit. Not surprisingly my source also mentioned seeing former President George. W. Bush and the former CIA Director, William Casey in the building. Busy place that FTD, n'est pa?

Now that you're nearly finished reading this book and will surely have some time on your hands until the next book is published, let me make a suggestion. Get on the net and type in "William Casey suspicious death." Although this is not my conspiracy theory it is one that will keep you thinking about Wright-Patterson, UFOs and the possibility that the government is still sitting on the greatest non-secret secret of all time – Evidence of Alien Visitation to Wright-Patterson and Beyond!

Corvette "Al"

"Al", who introduced me to the WPAFB alien topic, is now retired. He lightly edited our 43-year-old conversation appearing in this book. He's still a great All-American guy. Like all SES's he can neither confirm nor deny extraterrestrial visitation.

Final Words

The Danger of Wright-Patterson Armchair Research
"If you say you remember the 60's, then you weren't there" – Grace Slick, best known as the lead singer for the Jefferson Airplane.

There are several self-proclaimed "Wright-Patterson UFO experts" who write books and give regular lectures on that topic. Unfortunately for the consuming public, many of these individuals have, by their own admission, never set foot on this top secret property. As a result, while their works can contain some well-researched revelatory information, those works are often filled with puzzling misinformation that only further confounds an already confused public. The effect of this is as damaging to Ufology as the moronic babblings of debunkers who spew on about the magical powers of both Venus and weather balloons.

A case in point involves a well-known researcher and author who claimed in an IUFOC 2014 lecture that "Wright-Patterson Air Force Base **uses** nuclear power on the base!" Note the bolding of the word "uses." The presenter definitely used the present tense with obvious but unnecessary theatrical emphasis.

His is a factually false statement, spoken at that time in a dramatic tone meant to either vilify the US Air Force or create *only-the-speaker-knows* intrigue that just isn't there. As I sat thru the above presentation I recorded a page and a half of questionable statements that were made therein. I patiently waited for the Q & A session to get some clarification from the speaker, but conveniently the speaker allowed zero time for public cross-examination. I promptly complained to the event host, Alejandro Rojas, about the immediate need for a public questioning of the speaker but was turned down flat. I fumed then but decided to do my own fact checking before engaging the author and presenter, which I did over a year later at Contact in the Desert 2015.

While he sat at his book table, I introduced myself and my concerns with his book and presentation. I was pleasantly surprised that he took it like a man and asked for examples of the inaccuracies.

When I mentioned some of these, his early defense was "I was talking about the 50's, 60's and 70's." That defense collapsed when I told him about the now decommissioned nuclear reactor at the base, how easy it was for a fact checker to establish the truth about the reactor, and his totally erroneous "*uses* nuclear power" accusation.

WPAFB nuclear facility erroneously reported as *active* in 2014 by researchers whose fact checking failed.

Lest the conference presenter claim it was an inadvertent slip of the tongue, which can and often does happen in front of large audiences, I quote the conference website's description of said presentation. "The physical evidence of extraterrestrial visitation was buried deep within this nuclear stronghold." I think we can rule out a nuclear "slip of the tongue", don't you?

In his defense, the author graciously invited me to review his book and to tell him where the mistakes were made. I promised to read it and provide feedback to the authors.

Meanwhile, the nuclear reactor in question is located in building 470 in Area B. It was completed in 1965, used by the Air Force Institute of Technology for a couple of years, and then officially decommissioned on 1 July 1971. A fact sheet containing historical details of the reactor can be found on the Wright-Patterson public website and has been there since at least March 2011, long enough for the authors of the Area 51 and Wright-Patterson book to have found it prior to their publication. The only other nuclear possibility the authors could have been referencing, albeit still incorrectly, was the base's nuclear weapons storage area which was active from 1960 through 1975. This fact would still not justify the presenter's dramatic and impugning accusation that "Wright-Patterson uses nuclear energy!"

After reading the book upon which the conference presentation was based, I contacted the authors in good faith to obtain clarification. The first author deferred my questions to his co-author who, in-turn, asked for a month's delay to respond to those questions. After a month's delay still no response. Perhaps their reluctance to communicate is due to the fact that I pointedly asked if an important event in their book "could have been fabricated out of whole cloth?"; since the person they were talking about in that event happened to be my boss at that time – the WPAFB Base Commander. When I presented my former boss with the book quote attributed to him by the authors he denied any knowledge of it. More damaging to the story, he insists *not* having a conversation with a named Colonel whom the authors say acted as their emissary to the Commander's office. Finally, despite *dramatically* quoting him in their book, the authors failed to get the Commanders name correct, both his first and his last! Someone in that story is not telling the truth. Who could that be? If it is the authors, even J. Allen Hynek who misinformed the public for decades would deeply frown upon this UFO fairytale.

Yes, Linda, There Is A Santa Claus

Timing is everything in life. Long after my car wreck I calculated that had I been in the fateful intersection two tenths of a second sooner I would most likely be dead. That is because the car I hit would have hit me instead, directly in my driver's door with his huge vintage Cadillac. Just imagine the loss of humanity!

If Linda Moulton Howe asks me the $1 million question once again, "Did you see any aliens at Wright-Patt", I'm now going to have to tell her "Yes." Maybe not the exact kind she's looking for, but aliens nonetheless.

Tipped off by a longtime friend and fellow marathoner I had recently bumped into at the gym, I discovered that an alien has been kept in a jar in a classified room in Area B at Wright-Patt for the last several years. Although my friend had personally never seen the alien himself, Steve had heard about it through the "WPAFB network", the same employee network that has kept the Wright-Patterson alien story alive for decades.

A day after initially talking to Steve he emailed me the alien caretaker's name and email address. I contacted the caretaker, "Shelley", and set up an appointment to come see her little friend and get some background information.

It took a few weeks of on-again, off-again appointments but we were finally able to synchronize our schedules and meet on a beautiful mid-September morning in the lobby of Building 557 in Area B. The entrance to the building is flanked by large scale models of the programs which are managed in that complex of buildings.

This alien has been stowed in a classified room for years.

As soon as I stepped into the lobby there was Shelley and "Al Ian Grey" as I call it, comfortably reposed in a see-through yellow plastic container about 6 inches in diameter an 8 inches tall. The red "Radioactive" stickers jumped out at me immediately and I wondered aloud to Shelley if we needed to call the HazMat team for immediate emergency assistance. She assured me it was harmless and if not, didn't we all need a third arm for those cocktail parties whose guests wish they had an extra one after picking up an hors d'oeurvre plate and a glass of wine.

Yes, we took the lid off and no one has died, yet.

For the next hour Shelley peppered me with a constant stream of outstanding UFO/ET related questions while I tried to take photos and learn more about her small friend's provenance. Eventually we got into a rhythm and traded relatively even amounts of questions and answers.

To the best of her knowledge, the alien was originally owned by a man we'll call "Jayman" who worked in the Air Force Material Command Public Affairs Office. I discovered a few articles he wrote while in that particular office available on the internet which verified his employment in Public Affairs.

Using the Wright-Patt network, I found Jayman's former co-workers who promised to pass along my contact information and my desire to speak with him about his former protégé in a jar. After a few weeks of silence I finally received an email from Jayman containing but a single sentence of explanation regarding his compact cosmic comrade.

234

Eventually Jayman's Al Ian Grey was spotted by Mr. Mike "P" who was Shelley's boss. Mike expressed a great deal of interest in Al Ian Grey and was eventually given custody by Jayman.

According to Shelley, it was widely known that Mike often took Al with him on visits to local pubs and other gathering spots as a conversation starter. As the author has not yet had a chance to talk with Mike about these activities they are not verified at this time. That said, there is no doubt that Al Ian Grey's presence, carefully resting next to your frosty beer mug with his big eyes and alien body, and would start any number of tantalizing conversations with a Wright-Patterson employee-owner.

As postulated earlier, timing is everything. Had I arrived at the gym just a few seconds later that day I would not have run into Steve who gave me the heads up on Al. This singular incident of discovering Al Ian Grey, more than any other in recent months, provides great hope for future revelations out of Wright-Patterson.

If I can discover such interesting Wright-Patterson UFO history just standing around at the gym, like the novelty alien in a jar, imagine what I can uncover when I get serious about an entirely new book devoted exclusively to the subject. Perhaps tap more deeply into the old Wright-Patt network and let some of its former employees finally tell the stories they've been sitting on for decades.

Oh, one more thing before I go. Jayman's one sentence email to me regarding Al Ian Grey was:

"I bought the alien in the container at a local gun and knife show."

That's an interesting story, Jayman, interesting indeed.

References

The references listed below are not an exhaustive list. Some have been intentionally withheld to protect sources and resources or at the request of a few sources themselves.

Contributing Personal Discussions/Correspondence

The following notable individuals had personal discussions with the author and/or exchanged correspondence with the author on the primary topics in this book.

Corvette 'Al'
Gerald Anderson
John Burroughs
Art Campbell
Renee Carkin
Steve Colbern
Paul Davids
Preston Dennett
Stanton T. Friedman
Rosemary Ellen Guiley
Patty Greer
"Jayman"
"Shelley"
Linda Moulton Howe
Daryl Mayer
"Morley"
Jim Penniston
Nick Pope
Arthur Russell
Stephen C. Smith
Yvonne R. Smith
Jennifer Stein
Travis Walton

Books – Primary Relevance

Berlitz, Charles and William L. Moore. *The Roswell Incident.* New York, NY: Grossett & Dunlap, 1980. Print.
Campbell, Art. *Finding the UFO Crash at San Augustin.* Medford, Oregon: Minuteman Press, 2014. Print

Dolan, Richard. *UFOs and the National Security State, Chronology of a Cover Up, 1947-1973.* Newburyport, MA: Hampton Roads Publishing, 2002. Print.

Friedman, Stanton T. and Don Berliner. *Crash at Corona.* New York: Marlowe Company, Second Edition, 1994. Print.

Fuller, John G. *Incident at Exeter.* New York, NY: G. P. Putnam's Sons, 1966. Print

Lynott, Mark J. *Geographical Surveys at Two Earthen Mound Sites, Wright-Patterson Air Force Base Ohio.* U.S.A.: 1997. Print.

Pope, Nick, John Burroughs, and Jim Penniston. *Encounter in Rendlesham Forest.* New York, NY: Thomas Dunne Books, 2014. Print

Ruppelt, Edward J. *The Report on Unidentified Flying Objects.* U.S.A.: Doubleday & Co., 1956. Print.

Walton, Travis. *Fire In The Sky.* Snowflake, AZ: Skyfire Productions, 2010. Print

Warren, Larry and Peter Robbins. *Left at East Gate.* New York, NY: Marlowe & Co., 1997. Print.

Books – Secondary Relevance

Dolan, Richard. *UFOs and the National Security State, The Cover Up Exposed 1973-1991*. Rochester, NY: Keyhole Publishing Company, 2010. Print.

Edwards, Frank. *Flying Saucers, Serious Business*. New York, NY: Lyle Stuart Inc., 1966. Print.

Fawcett, Larry. Barry J. Greenwood. *The UFO Cover-Up*. New York, NY: Simon and Schuster, 1992. Print.

Fowler, Raymond E. *Casebook of a UFO Investigator*. Englewood Cliffs, NJ: Prentice-Hall, 1981. Print.

Friedman, Stanton T. *Top Secret/MAJIC*. Cambridge, MA: Da Capo Press, 2005. Print.

Hopkins, Budd. *Intruders*. New York, NY: Random House, Inc., 1987. Print.

Jacobs, David M. *Secret Life*. New York, NY: Simon and Schuster, 1992. Print.

Jacobsen, Annie. *AREA 51, An Uncensored History of America's Top Secret Military Base*. New York, NY: Little, Brown & Company, 2011. Print.

Leir, Roger Dr. *Alien Implants*. New York, NY: Dell Publishing, 2000. Print.

Marrs, Jim. *Alien Agenda*. New York, NY: Harper Collins, 1998. Print.

Pope, Nick. *Open Skies, Closed Minds*. Woodstock, NY: The Overlook Press, Peter Mayer Publishers, Inc, 1999. Print.

Smith, Yvonne R. *Coronado, The President, The Secret Service and Alien Abductions.* U.S.A.: 2014. Print.

Spencer, John. Hillary Evans. *Phenomenon, Forty Years of Flying Saucers.* New York, NY: Avon Books, 1989. Print.

Strieber, Whitley. *Communion.* New York, NY: Avon Books, 1988. Print.

Sturrock, Peter A. *The UFO Enigma.* New York, NY: Warner Books, 1999. Print.

Torres, Noe. Ruben Uriate. *Mexico's Roswell.* U.S.A.: 2008. Print.

Conference Presentations (Attended)

Greer, Patty. "Crop Circles & The Real Circle Makers." International UFO Congress, Open Minds. We-Ko-Pa Resort, Fountain Hills, AZ, February 2015. Conference presentation.

Knapp, George. "Area 51's Whistleblower." International UFO Congress, Open Minds. We-Ko-Pa Resort, Fountain Hills, AZ, February 2015. Conference presentation.

Lamb, Barbara. "ET/Human Hybrids: Are They Real and Are They Here?" International UFO Congress, Open Minds. We-Ko-Pa Resort, Fountain Hills, AZ, February 2013. Conference presentation.

Lazar, Bob. "Special Q&A Session with Bob Lazar." International UFO Congress, Open Minds. We-Ko-Pa Resort, Fountain Hills, AZ, February 2015. Conference presentation.

Leir, Dr. Roger and Steve Colbern. "Alien Implants, The Tip of the Iceberg." International UFO Congress, Open Minds. We-Ko-Pa Resort, Fountain Hills, AZ, February 2013. Conference presentation.

Schmitt, Donald. "Inside the Real Area 51: The Secret History of Wright-Patterson." International UFO Congress, Open Minds. We-Ko-Pa Resort, Fountain Hills, AZ, 13 February, 2014. Conference presentation.

Schroeder, Robert. "How Modern Physics is Revealing the Technology of UFOs." International UFO Congress, Open Minds. We-Ko-Pa Resort, Fountain Hills, AZ, February 2014. Conference presentation.

Sprinkle, Dr. Leo. "Memories of an ET Experiencer and Spiritual Pigtailer." International UFO Congress, Open Minds. We-Ko-Pa Resort, Fountain Hills, AZ, February 2013. Conference presentation.

Walton, Travis. Yvonne Smith, Kathleen Marden, Victoria Gavoian, Sherry Wilde, Robert Perala. "Contact Experience Panel." Contact in the Dessert Conference. Joshua Tree Retreat Center, Joshua Tree, CA, May 2015. Conference presentation.

Walton, Travis. Yvonne Smith, Dr. Lynne Kitei, Roberta Perala, Celeste Yarnell. "Contact Experience Panel." Contact in the Dessert Conference. Joshua Tree Retreat Center, Joshua Tree, CA, 10 August 2014. Conference presentation.

Conference Presentations (DVD)

Burroughs, John and Pat Frascogna. *The Rendlesham Case.* International UFO Congress, Open Minds. We-Ko-Pa Resort, Fountain Hills, AZ, 22 February, 2015. Conference presentation DVD. Open Minds.

Government Documents

Wright-Patterson Air Force Base, Building Location Plan, Date: 23 December 1947, Updated: 3 May 1948. Approved by: J. F. Klentzman, Captain, USAF, Air Installation Officer.

National Museum of the US Air Force Research Division, Blue Book Reports, Document #'s 70-152-1 through 70-152-8

National Register of Historic Places, Inventory – Nomination Form. Wright-Patterson Air Force Base Mound, 23 February 1972.

Newspaper Articles

Anthrax Not Found, Bryan Times, Associated Press, James Hannah, 9 December 1995

Ghost Stories: Workers say they see spirits roaming building's hall. Skywriter, 25 October 1996.

Events spur AF base to call in 'Ghost Hunters', Stars and Stripes, Lisa Burgess, 26 February 2008

Movies

Fire in the Sky. Dir. Robert Lieberman. Paramount Pictures, 1993. Recorded film.

Roswell, The U.F.O. Coverup. Dir. Jeremy Kagan. Viacom Pictures, 1994. DVD

Television Shows

"Military Vs. UFOs", UFO Hunters. History Channel. 27 February 2008. Television.

"Area 51 Revealed", UFO Hunters. History Channel. 25 February 2009. Television.

"The Real Roswell", UFO Hunters. History Channel. 3 December 2008. Television.

"The Silencers", UFO Hunters. History Channel. 29 October 2009. Television.

"UFO Surveillance." UFO Hunters. History Channel. 20 May 2009. Television.

"Rendlesham Forest." Alien Mysteries. Discovery Channel. 10 March 2013.

Archives Consulted

University of Arizona Archives. James McDonald Collection. Tucson, AZ.

National Museum of the United States Air Force Research Division Archives. Wright-Patterson Air Force Base, Ohio.

Technical Reports and Papers

Analysis Report on Metal Sample from Sphere. Author: Steve Colbern, 21 February, 2009

Anatomical anomalies in crop formation plants. Author: W.C. Leavengood, 1994.

Archeology, Geomorphy, and Land Use History at WPAFB, Ohio, Report #389. Great Lakes Archeological Research Center (GLARC), 1995.

Podcasts

Col. Charles Halt and John Burroughs Hash It Out. Dark Matters Podcast, 10 December 2014

Web Publications

Enoch, Nick. *Beam me up, sporty! UFO spotted among fireworks at Olympics opening ceremony.* The Daily Mail: Published: 11:01 EST, 30 July 2012 | Updated: 05:31 EST, 31 July 2012. Last accessed: 10/15/2015. http://www.dailymail.co.uk/news/article-2181066/Olympics-2012-UFO-sighted-Games-opening-ceremony.html. Web.

Crestleaf. *Obituary, Russell, Clyde.* Last accessed: 10/16/2015. http://crestleaf.com/p/50ba94d6651a69e4d473a3f1/clyde-russell. Web.

Robinson, Larry. *Solving the 1965 Exeter, NH, Sightings.* Updated 06/18/13. Last accessed: 10/16/2015. http://midimagic.sgc-hosting.com/howiextr.htm. Web.

Brown, Joel. *N.H. Teen's 1965 Sighting Became Blueprint for UFOs.* http://www.ufocasebook.com/exeterrevisited.html. Last accessed: 10/16/2015. Original article: Brown, Joel. Boston Globe, 01/09/2005, *Close Encounter Revisited.* http://www.boston.com/news/local/articles/2005/09/01/close_en counter_revisited/. Web.

UFO Blogger. *History Channel - Rendlesham Forest UFO Binary Code Decoded But Decipher Is Wrong Says, Jim Penniston.* http://www.ufo-blogger.com/2011/02/rendlesham-forest-binary-code.html. Last accessed 10/16/2015. Web.

Cohen, Jerry. The Rendlesham Forest UFO Case - Another Perspective. http://www.cohenufo.org/CombinedRendlesham.htm. Last updated: 8/18/2011. Last Accessed: 10/16/2015. Web.

The Rendlesham Forest Incident - Official Website. http://www.therendleshamforestincident.com/. All pages read. Last accessed: 10/16/2015

The UFO Briefing Document Case Histories. *1980: UFO Incidents at Rendlesham Forest, England.* http://www.bibliotecapleyades.net/ciencia/ufo_briefingdocument/1980.htm. Last accessed: 10/16/2015. Web.

The Rendlesham Incident. *2010 Landing Site.* http://www.therendleshamincident.co.uk/2010-landing-site/. Last accessed: 10/16/2015. Web

Price, Geoff. UFO Evidence. *The Travis Walton UFO Abduction Case.* http://www.ufoevidence.org/documents/doc347.htm. Last accessed: 10/16/2015. Web.

National Archives. *Unidentified Flying Objects - Project BLUE BOOK.* http://www.archives.gov/research/military/air-force/ufos.html. Last accessed: 10/17/2015. Web.

88th Air Base Wing Public Affairs. *Air Force Nuclear Engineering Center at Wright-Patterson Air Force Base.* Posted 3/18/2011. Last accessed:10/16/2015. http://www.wpafb.af.mil/library/factsheets/factsheet.asp?id=18061 Web.

Robinson, J. Dennis. *Norman Muscarello Recounts His Incident At Exeter.* http://www.seacoastnh.com/famous-people/link-free-or-die/norman-muscarello-recalls-his-ufo-incident-at-exeter/. SeaCoastNH.com. Last accessed 10/16/2015. Web.

Glossary

AAF – Army Air Force
ABW – Air Base Wing
AFRL – Air Force Research Laboratory
CIA – Central Intelligence Agency
CITD – Contact In The Desert
CYA – Cover Your Ass
DOD – Department of Defense
EPA – Environmental Protection Agency
ET – Extraterrestrial
FS – Forest Service
FTD – Foreign Technology Division
GLARC – Great Lakes Archeological Research Center
GS – General Schedule
HazMat – Hazardous Material
IUFOC – International UFO Congress
MIB – Men In Black
MiG – Mikoyan-Gurevich Design Bureau
NASIC – National Air and Space Intelligence Center
PA – Public Affairs
PACL – Public Affairs Entertainment Liaison
PhD – Doctorate
RAAF – Roswell Army Air Field
RAF – Royal Air Force
SciFi – Science Fiction
SECAF – Secretary of the Air Force
SES – Senior Executive Service
Syfy – Science Fiction Channel
UAP – Unidentified Aerial Phenomena
UFO – Unidentified Flying Object
UK – United Kingdom
WP – Wright-Patterson
WPAFB – Wright-Patterson Air Force Base
Wright-Patt – Wright-Patterson
WTF – What The F@ck

Index

A

B

C

D

E

247

Twizzlers, 115, 116, 118

The author's Department of Defense Civil Service career spanned
five decades at Wright-Patterson Air Force Base from 1973 until
2011 when he retired as a Senior Electronics Engineer. While on a
two-year Executive Loan to the Wright-Patterson Base Commander,
he served as the first Director of the Installation Civilian Wellness
Program managing activities and scientific studies affecting 10,000
base civilian employees. As Chairman of the Ada Joint Program
Office's Evaluation and Validation Team he managed software
developments critical to the National Defense. An avid runner and
golfer, he has finished 13 marathons, including two Boston's and
owns two holes-in-one – perfect symmetry! Contact him at:
ITSAUFO@Yahoo.com